FIGHT

Also from the Author

Work it Out Without a Workout

FIT TO FIGHT

THE COMPLETE MANUAL ON SELF-DEFENSE FOR WOMEN

VESNA P. JACOB

RANDOM HOUSE INDIA

Published by Random House India in 2014
1

Copyright © Vesna P. Jacob 2014

Random House Publishers India Private Limited
Windsor IT Park, 7th Floor
Tower-B, A-1, Sector-125
Noida 201301, UP

Random House Group Limited
20 Vauxhall Bridge Road
London SW1V 2SA
United Kingdom

978 81 8400 449 6

This book is sold subject to the condition that it shall not, by way of trade or otherwise, be lent, resold, hired out, or otherwise circulated without the publisher's prior consent in any form of binding or cover other than that in which it is published and without a similar condition including this condition being imposed on the subsequent purchaser.

Typeset in Sabon by R. Ajith Kumar

Photographs © Md Sabi

Printed and bound in India by Replika Press Private Limited

For my daughter Daniela
and
To all daughters

'In your light I learn how to love. In your beauty,
how to make poems. You dance inside my chest
where no one sees you, but sometimes I do,
and that sight becomes this art.'
—*Rumi*

All suggestions and opinions in this work are personal and those of the author. A Stun Gun (mentioned on p. 49–50) cannot be used without a license from the requisite authority as mentioned under the Arms Act, 1959.

Contents

Note to Reader		ix
Prologue		xi
Crimes Against Women		xv
1	Pre-empt, Prepare, Avoid	1
2	Possible Scenarios	8
3	Your House and You	19
4	Harassing Calls and the Internet	25
5	Meeting for the First Time and Dating	28
6	Waiting	37
7	Get Involved!	40
8	Weapons to Defend Yourself	46
9	Soft Targets	61
10	Martial Arts and Self-defense Techniques	76
11	Basic Self-defense Moves Everyone Should Know	91
12	Fit and Strong	132
13	What If…	155
14	Worst Comes to Worst	162

Appendix 1: Safety Apps	177
Appendix 2: Women's Helpline Numbers and NGOs	183
Appendix 3: Police Helpline Numbers	206
Appendix 4: Laws and Acts Under the Indian Penal Code (IPC)	222
Appendix 5: References	230
Acknowledgements	235
A Note on the Author	237

Dear Reader,

This book has been inspired by a number of unfortunate, spine-chilling events that shook India, starting with the gang rape of a 24-year-old medical student Jyoti, better known as Nirbhaya, in December 2012. Her ordeal was a wake-up call to so many of us, and her heroic fight and will to survive moved the nation to take action and change the system. Unfortunately, Nirbhaya is not the only one who has endured/s such atrocity; her case was just the first layer of the Pandora's box, which was opened with her demise.

The incidents have not stopped. Every day we still read and hear about so many other nameless girls who get kidnapped, molested, and raped. Some survive, many don't. Being a mother, I find it particularly difficult to comprehend the crimes against children who are the most vulnerable and become an easy prey for perpetrators.

This book is my way of taking action. I want to equip you with basic self-defense tips, to urge you to become more careful, to try and pre-empt possibly dangerous situations, and whenever possible to avoid being in any danger. Least

Note to Reader

of all, I want to give you information which may be useful in getting you out of a dangerous situation with least harm.

Through the course of the book I will be sharing some of my personal stories as well as stories of other women who have had dangerous encounters and been in unpleasant situations. Let's be frank, a majority of women (regardless of our background or country of origin) have experienced some sort of unpleasant situation during our lifetime—from 'eve teasing', groping, drug-laced drinks to other crimes such as molestation or rape.

My sincere wish to you, my reader, is that you may never need to use any of the information given here. But it is always better to be ready. Remember, preparation is half the battle won.

Love and light,

Vesna

Prologue

Tuzla, Bosnia and Herzegovina

I was just a little bit over 16 years old when this happened. One of my girlfriends had a nasty fight with a boy she was madly in love with, and I was looking for her to console her. It was a warm summer evening and I went looking for her in one of her favourite places—the terrace of the building she lived in. When I got there, I found her boyfriend there instead, whom I knew because of her. He invited me to step out onto the terrace and I saw an opportunity to play peacemaker and get them back together. I accepted the invitation in good faith and went to the terrace. Somewhere in the back of my head I registered that he had taken too much time closing the door behind me, but it didn't raise any alarms in my head.

We started talking. I listened to his monologue of how much he loved her and how he couldn't imagine his life without her in it. However, there was something strange about his behaviour; he would occasionally, for a moment, look at me with his eyes glazed as if he had a fever. I didn't want to take any chances and I excused myself saying that it was getting late and I should get going. He didn't object, but as I was walking away he mumbled something like 'let's see how far you get'. The comment didn't make sense and only when I reached the door and noticed that the handle had been removed was I truly alarmed. I realized that it must have been him who had removed the handle after me. The next moment he grabbed me and threw me against the wall and was inching towards me with glazed eyes.

Once I got over my initial shock I became angry. I started shouting at him: who did he think he was, and what the hell did he think he was doing! He responded by ordering me to be quiet. I started screaming and calling for help instead and only stopped when he shouted back and slammed his fist into the wall and started bleeding. He just didn't seem like the person I knew, but instead appeared to be some kind of lunatic who was going to hurt me. I covered my face with my hands while my mind raced. I started to plead with him, 'You don't seem to know what you are doing, and you don't really want to hurt me.' I reminded him that I was his friend, that he loved his girlfriend, and that this was not the way to win her back. It seemed to work better than me screaming. He moved away from me a bit and kept on saying that it was true, that he would have never hurt me. Just then, he fell and all of a sudden started shaking with his eyes rolling upwards. He was having some sort of a seizure!

I took this as an opportunity to escape and ran to the door. I noticed that there was a rather large window right next to it. As I was fiddling with the door, trying to open it, he grabbed me again and threw me back against the wall. I tried pleading with him, but this time it didn't work. I covered my face with my hands and looked for an opportunity to physically fight him, try to hit him in the groin and get away. I made up my mind that I would jump through the window as that seemed like the only option left and hoped that I wouldn't get cut badly.

As he dragged me far away from the door, I saw some empty bottles of alcohol and some pills spilt all over the terrace and made up my mind to try one more time to talk to him. I told him that I knew this is not who he really was, that he was drunk and high and would regret his actions once he sobered up. This somehow brought him to his senses again. He started to apologize one moment and then the very next moment he would again have that crazed look in his eyes, and then all of the sudden he had a seizure again. I ran as fast as I could to the door, but this time I kept watching him all the while. I had given myself one more attempt at opening the door and in the event he recovered and got up, that I would have enough time to break the window and escape or at least alarm the neighbours. Luckily this time I managed to open the door and run away, leaving his shivering body behind. I ran all the way to my house, frequently looking behind me, imagining and fearing he was going to grab me and pull me back again.

By the time I reached home I was shivering, my heart was racing, and I couldn't comprehend what had just happened. To make it even worse I had this overwhelming feeling that I had brought this upon myself. That I was responsible for what had just happened to me. Why did I have to step out onto the terrace? Why didn't I see what he was doing with the door? Why didn't I fight more successfully? Why didn't I break the glass the first time?

After this incident, I stopped going out for quite some time, refusing to take calls from my friends. I also never uttered a word about it to my parents and tried to erase and severe all connections from the people from that day in my attempt to disconnect myself from that event. Even though I did not technically get assaulted, I felt terribly violated and feared what could have happened to me had I not managed to escape. I had feelings ranging between horror, despair, shame, and helpless anger. I lived with this feeling for a few years.

In turn, I started reading a lot about women who were assaulted and how they coped with it. One thing that stood out prominently was that they all had a similar feeling of guilt, anger, and shame. Consequently a chilling realization came over me—that I was not the only one going through the same nightmare. I was not alone.

Crimes Against Women

Crimes against women are increasing everyday in the form of various kinds of sexual assaults. These have triggered many social discussions about the safety and security of women in general—what needs to be done regarding the prevention and protection of more 'vulnerable' groups of women, for example, women working late, or in shifts, single women who live alone, college going students and young women who go out and stay out late, etc. There are grossly misinformed people who say that if a woman has been attacked it is somehow her fault. What is even more disturbing is that even well meaning persons while commenting or offering solutions indirectly imply that a woman who has been abused brings it upon herself either by dressing in a certain way, or going out after dark, or indulging in 'risky' behaviour. The onus always seems to be on women to not 'provoke' or 'entice' men to attack them. Well, let me establish one thing clearly: IT IS NEVER YOUR FAULT.

Being harassed or sexually assaulted, right from being 'eve-teased', groped, stalked, to being raped regardless of the circumstances under which the crime was committed, even if it was done in the middle of the night, even if the girl was out alone, even if she put herself in a 'dangerous position', no one has the right to touch her without her consent. According to a study done by the Rape and Abuse Incest National Network (RAINN), sexual assault in the United States takes place every 2 minutes. Statistics from the National Crime Record Bureau (NCRB) India show that a rape takes place every 20 minutes somewhere in India. According to the same organization, crimes against women have increased by 7.1 percent in the last three years, and child rape cases have increased by 336 percent in the last 10 years. This kind of statistics is also due to the increase of reporting cases of sexual violence. Shockingly, in 67 percent cases, the attacker is known to the victim, so it is more likely that the assaults are done by someone you know rather than a complete stranger. According to the FBI, rape is the most brutal and traumatic crime second only to murder. The victim has to cope not only with the physical trauma but also undergoes emotional trauma, which can lead to many psychological problems ranging from phobias, sleep disorders, intimacy issues, panic attacks, guilt, and reliving the event. If we add the social stigma to this, you can only imagine what it must be to live after such a crime.

Due to social stigma, many sexual assault crimes go unreported even in developed countries such as the United

States; studies have shown that only 30 to 50 percent of rapes get reported—one can only imagine what the reality is back home. One of the positive developments following the horrifying Nirbhaya incident was that it brought society and media's attention to this acute problem, and also encourage other rape victims to go public and talk about and report rapes. Even though the media attention on the incident faded after a while, the incident inspired many to take action and promote start campaigns to fight gender inequality, female foeticide, and promote equality in the workplace. All these efforts are welcomed and necessary in re-educating society regarding the treatment of women and children. However, this is a process which may take many years to take root and change society and people's mindset (remember we are trying to change a mindset which has been pervasive for centuries). In the meantime, we need to be practical and equip ourselves with enough knowledge and techniques to protect ourselves and our right to live.

Note: In real life an attacker could be either male or female and the victim could be male as well as a female, but for the clarity of this book the victim is portrayed as female and the attacker as male.

Pre-empt, Prepare, Avoid

Defend (your)self

There are many myths and misconceptions about self-defense. A common one is that you can successfully defend yourself only if you are a martial arts specialist who has spent many years practicing various techniques and grips. Another one is that women are too weak to defend themselves. And yet another is that self-defense refers only to the physical aspect of defending your life. I have to admit that I went for self-defense classes with the aim to learn how to kick some butt. My opinion being that if someone attacks you, he deserves to get hurt, right?

Well, the philosophy of True Self-Defense is far from all of this. Yes, it will teach you techniques to defend yourself (even if you are not a martial arts specialist), but it will also teach you something much deeper and more pragmatic—it will focus on steps BEFORE any physical attack happens. The perfect self-defense pre-empts things so far ahead that ideally the situation where you need to defend yourself doesn't arise at all.

Pre-empt, Prepare, Avoid (PPA)

Whenever possible avoid dangerous situation. Yes, I know this sounds obvious, but the true meaning of this is usually completely misunderstood because people generally understand this as blaming the victim, i.e., if she finds herself in danger it is something *she* has gotten herself into and she is to blame. Being attacked and molested is NEVER your fault. But you can prepare yourself and be ready for any dangerous situation that may arise.

Step 1: I want you to start observing your environment, looking out for potential threats even if there is nothing obviously wrong happening around you. I want you to change your perspective and look at things and situations as potentially dangerous or not dangerous. Next, whatever you have labelled as 'potentially dangerous' are the things you need to prepare yourself against. This can be applied to pretty much any situation in your life—whether you are going to or from some place (office, gym, club), walking on the street, parking or getting into the car, walking into the building, meeting someone for the first time, online friendships, etc.

So, how do you prepare yourself?

I am not going to lie to you. In the beginning, this will require quite a bit of mental reprogramming. I want you to start seeing possible threats in everything around you. It is a bit unnerving to do but it is necessary. When you look at your surroundings with a fresh pair of eyes, you'll soon discover that there are threats everywhere and this realization is not going to be a pleasant one. Having said that, remember that this is a necessary part of your training. With regular practice your instincts will get honed and you should be able to distinguish real threats.

Looking Up

The very first thing you need to do is start looking around. I have noticed many girls walking with their heads down, completely ignoring the world around them. Then there are a vast majority of girls who spend their time fiddling with their phones, not paying any attention to things happening around them. I assume the picture they want to portray is someone busy and minding their own business. Many of us go for a jog in the park, or walk on the street with headphones on. Unfortunately, the problem with being preoccupied in public is that you may walk straight into danger and once you realize you are in it, you will have no plan B on how to get out of it. **Remember, if you pretend not to see them, it does not mean they don't see you.** On the contrary, perpetrators look for the girls who are unaware, the ones who are not paying any attention to their surrounding—this makes them an easy target.

Be Aware! Be Alert!

Be aware of everything around you and your environment.
- Are there people on the street?
- Have you noticed anyone paying you any extra attention?
- Do you have to pass by them?
- Is it a well-lit area that you need to cross?
- Are there any pockets of shadows/trees/bushes in your path?
- Could somebody be hiding in these pockets without you seeing them?
- Is there an alternative way?
- Is there anything on the street that can be used as a weapon, e.g. glass, sticks, stones, etc.?
- Are there any obstacles/objects on the street which can be used to distract or hide behind or run around?

Being alert means taking off your headphones and listening. Even if you do not see someone, you may be able to hear footsteps behind you or some sound or movement behind the car. It stands to reason to be even more vigilant at night as there are usually more people around during daytime and visibility and shadows are not a problem then.

Once you have assessed the area ahead of you, you need to estimate how to brace/prepare yourself for any potential situations. I have found **Jeff Cooper's colour coding** particularly useful in getting yourself psychologically ready for any potential situation. Jeff Cooper was a United States Marine who adopted Marine states of readiness. Marine Coding for States of Readiness is colour coding method which helps soldiers be more aware and better prepared for an attack or a battle by indicating possibility and imminence of the attack. Jeff had used this coding to condition one's mind and the mind's perception of potential danger. Simply put, this is a method where you allocate a certain colour to the danger perceived in a particular situation.

The colour code of a perceived danger is as following:

- **White—no perceived danger:** This is a state of complete lack of awareness and no perception of danger. Unaware and unprepared. If you get attacked in this state, you will probably freeze as there will be too many things to process at the same time.
- **Yellow—there could be a possibility of a threat:** This state is also called 'Relaxed Alertness'. This means that you are aware of your environment, but nothing and no one in particular is drawing your attention, however you are observing your environment (including the areas behind you) like a scanning radar. Your thoughts are 'today I could be defending myself'. State Yellow should be the state you spend most of your time in as it keeps you aware of your environment and open to early detections of threat. You should ALWAYS be in the yellow state when in unknown places or surrounded by people you do not know.

- **Orange—possible and probable threat/attack:** There is something wrong with the entire situation you are in and you can see danger coming from a specific area or person. It is also called 'Specific Alertness'. Here you are readying yourself for the eventual fight, considering your options, exits and strategies. At this point, you need to determine the trigger which will give you a signal to switch and transit into State Red, which is the fight state.
- **Red—immediate danger/under an attack:** So a person X has done what you have set as your trigger and the fight is on. You are now defending yourself.

Colour coding is important and useful as it mentally prepares you for what is to come and helps you brace yourself for the next step.

Imagine walking on a street and there is a group of people on one side. You are already in State Yellow; your body language and facial expressions are relaxed, but you are aware of your environment and observing the situation. As you get closer to them, you notice that they are standing next to a shadowed area where you could be pulled in. The moment you detect a possible specific danger you should enter State Orange. Here you are strategizing, looking for other options—perhaps it is better that you cross the road and walk on the other side. Keep an eye on them discretely and scan the area looking for alternative ways out. If they don't pay you any attention you can go back to State Yellow—Relaxed Alertness. I would take it one notch further; before walking alone on a street, I suggest keeping a key or a pen in your hand and hold a cell phone on speed dial to call for help if required. You should also look for stones, bottles, and dirt as all of that can become quite effective weapons. Another thing is that your body language should be one of determination. Head up, back straight, and the eyes looking around and aware. In case the group of people starts giving you any unwanted attention, you need to switch back to State Orange, observe your environment more closely for weapons and exits and decide on the trigger in your mind. If any of the men start crossing the street and walking towards you change your direction and retrace your steps, walking back to where you came from and if they start following or running after you, you need to be in State Red and ready to fight. This may sound quite melodramatic and in all probability none of those of men may even give you a second look, but just in case they do, you have pre-empted the situation and had prepared yourself. As far as the choice of your actions and 'weapons' go, we will discuss it further in another chapter.

Possible Scenarios

Fight or Flight

Before we look at different possible scenarios, let us talk about why it is so important to pre-empt a situation. Most of you may have heard of the **'Fight or Flight'** response. It is also called Acute Stress Response. It is a physiological reaction in presence of something life-threatening and terrifying physically (for example, being attacked) or mentally (being really scared). What happens internally is that our hypothalamus triggers the sympathetic nervous system as well as the adrenal-cortical system which releases a number of reactions and hormones, all taking place in a blink of an eye. In turn, our pupils dilate, pulse quickens, muscles contracts due to blood rush and glucose release—all non essential systems slow down to provide additional blood to the major muscles, while smooth muscles relax, enabling more oxygen to the lungs. In other words, the brain stops focusing on the small tasks and concentrates on the bigger picture. In layman terms, fight or flight is the body's natural, primal response to a life-threatening situation that gears the body to either fight or run for its life.

You have probably heard about people who in situations of extreme danger—especially when their life depends on it or when they have been badly wounded—have been able to perform extremely well, even heroically at times, showing immense courage and strength. When later asked about the event, they generally say that they were not really thinking but simply trying to stay alive. On the other hand, we have all heard of situations in which people in the face of danger just froze out of fright and were unable to move, think, or react. Honestly, there is no way of knowing which way we will react in situations of extreme danger so the closest we can get ourselves to react the way we want is to prepare ourselves in advance and train our bodies so that if we are ever in a life-threatening situation the fear doesn't completely freeze us and prevents us from reacting.

Things to remember

- Assessing the area around you
- Looking for potential dangerous spots and eventually alternative exits

When in Your Car

Driving a car on your own is a huge convenience. It means you are not dependent on others for transport, especially late at night. However, as a driver there are a few things to consider for your personal safety.

In case your car breaks down at night, lock your car and stay put. Immediately call for help. Incidentally, if you are not aware of the ICE initiative, it is time you did. ICE is an acronym that stands for **'In Case of Emergency'**. The first three numbers on speed dial on your mobile should be of people who you can depend on to come and assist you at any given time. You can also set up a 'code word', which will be a signal for your contact that you are in danger. Switch on your hazard lights and wait for help. If you subscribe to an emergency breakdown service, call them as well and try and get your emergency contact to be with you as they arrive.

If you make slight contact with another car and there is very little traffic on the road or it is very late at night, don't stop. It could be an innocent bump or someone trying to simulate an accident to make you stoop and get you out of the car. Off course, I am not advising you to 'hit and run' but I want you to be prepared and aware of the possibility of danger and take a call accordingly.

Parking Lots

There are two aspects of a parking lot environment that you should keep in mind.

Are you the one parking the car or are you entering an already parked car?

If you are parking the car during the daytime, try to think ahead and figure out when you are getting back into the car. Is it going to be dark then?

> Choose the parking spot accordingly. If you are parking the car at night, always try to park in a well-lit area; avoid dark secluded corners or places close to bushes or trees.

If you are parking your car in an underground parking then remember that many underground parking lots have specially reserved places for women drivers—make use of them. If that is not the case, then try to park the car close to the elevator or the entrance/exit. Once you have parked the car, do not leave right away. First, assess the area around you, if this is in front of your building or house, have your keys ready—you don't want to end up standing in front of your house in the middle of the night trying to dig out a set of keys from your cluttered bag.

When getting into your car, look around you. Have your car key ready in advance, and the moment you enter the car, lock yourself in right away. Most women have a tendency of getting into the car and spending time sorting out papers or getting money out for parking or making a phone call before leaving the parking lot. Sitting in an unlocked car can give someone the opportunity to attack you.

In case there is a van or a SUV parked right next to your car, get into your car from the passenger side. We have all heard how often a girl is dragged into a larger car and driven away to a secluded spot to be assaulted. So a little inconvenience of entering through the passenger door is better than putting yourself in danger.

In case, you are walking through a parking lot and something does not seem right please go back into the mall or find a security guard and ask him to escort you to your car. Don't be embarrassed if you are scared; there's nothing wrong with being extra cautious.

Public Spaces

If you live in a high-rise building or work in one, remember that even if you are inside the premises you should not let your guard down. The problem with public or semi-public buildings is that you never know who might have gained access and how.

Elevators

When you are inside an elevator, observe the other people in it with you. Try and pay attention to see who has pushed which floor's button and if someone exits the elevator behind you when they were supposedly going to another floor. Also if you are the only girl /lady inside the elevator, try and position yourself close to the control panel and identify the alarm button at the very outset. Even if you feel threatened or are indeed threatened inside the elevator, do not push the red button as it will stop the elevator and trap you more effectively. Instead, push the floor button for the next floor so that you force the elevator doors to open.

Traveling by Air

Airports are large, busy public spaces with a lot of people transiting through them and with an equally large number of people working and waiting inside them. You never know who is reading your luggage tag and with what intent. So avoid putting your home address on the luggage tag—either put in your business card with a covered holder or place your business address inside your suitcase in case it gets lost.

Buses

When I started this section, I thought long and hard about what advice to give, since I am writing this post December 16, 2012. A lot of things came to mind. The first thought was that do I need to give someone guidelines about boarding public transport? But after what happened to Nirbhaya, I think there is a strong need to advise people, especially young women, to set up a few ground rules even about traveling by public transport.

Firstly, pay attention to the sign on the bus. Is it running as a normal service or is it is not supposed to be where it is? If is getting late and there are only a few people who don't necessarily look like passengers, think about waiting for the next bus. Now here lies the dilemma of whether to board a bus where your instincts tell you not to or risk waiting by the roadside which is also not always the most safe option in a lot of places around India. There is no easy answer for this, all I can say is trust your instincts and take a judgment call on the spot. If you are in a state-owned bus, try to sit next to the driver. If possible, avoid sitting next to the rear doors. Consider walking an extra distance if it means exiting near lit areas and try to avoid dark bus stops. While waiting for the bus, have your phone out and ready to call your ICE contact.

The other scenario regarding bus transportation is boarding a full bus. Most of the women I interviewed reported that their most traumatic experience was travelling on a bus while going to college and being groped pretty much by everyone who was in proximity to them. Most of them just tried to get out of harm's way—some got off as soon as they could, some tried not to give it too much attention, thinking it would pass and some started protesting and arguing and usually not being supported by anyone on the bus (women included). This sad situation has improved a bit. Girls are sticking together, traveling in groups and other women (and some men) do help in case of a problem. **If you enter a bus or train and you are groped, raise an alarm!**

Don't let him get away with it. Identify the person and ask other passengers not to be bystanders and to take action against him. Demand that he is taken off the bus or train. If none of this helps, you can always strike back using the techniques described in later chapters or you may opt to get away from the person and complain to the driver.

If you have a smartphone or any phone with a camera, you can take a photo of the offender and send it to the police using Facebook. You can call police or women helplines (see Appendix). Honestly speaking, even though the Criminal Law recognizes eve teasing and groping as offences I am not sure how helpful they can be in a given situation. However, exposing the perpetrator is a way of intimidating them, as most of them think they can get away with it.

Hitching Rides and Taxis

Hitching rides from strangers in today's world is an extremely dangerous option. World over, there have been many girls who have been raped after they have hitchhiked, taken the offer of a lift home with an acquaintance or a colleague or even someone they met in a party.

Unfortunately even flagging down a taxi or a charter cab is also not a safe option. There are enough dial-a-cab services available—make use of them but before getting into the cab, ask for the driver's name and note down the registration number of the cab. For added protection, SMS it to your trusted emergency contact. Check and opt for a cab service that has GPS tracking, and always insist on the meter being turned on—you might pay a little more but the moment the meter is running there is a record of the cab being engaged.

If you happen to be using a charter cab engaged by your company, insist that the company rules regarding female employees are followed. After the incidents that took place in Pune and Bangalore which resulted in the rape and murder of two women returning from work, clear guidelines regarding safety of transport have been adopted by most corporate entities. These include that a female passenger must not be left alone in the cab or be the last person to be dropped off. Even if someone else is in a hurry—don't let them get dropped before you! Your safety and security is more important than you wanting to be popular with your colleagues.

An interesting and dangerous story I heard was about a group of female students who had come from Central India to Delhi to study. Their first bus experience in Delhi was so awful that they decided to hitchhike through their college years! They told me that their bus experience was horrific—they were all badly groped, no one helped them, and even the driver took his own sweet time to stop the bus to let them out. They thought that it was safer to hitch a ride than take any public transport! Interestingly enough, they never had even a remotely dangerous situation while hitchhiking. But when I asked them if they would do it again, they said probably not and that even back then it was not as safe as they believed it was.

I must admit though that they had a few really good ground rules which they always followed.
1. They always moved in groups of a minimum three girls and never hitchhiked alone (one would flag down the ride and the others would just jump into the car).
2. They would never take a car with more than one person in it (in their words, one man meant that he would be too busy driving to be able to do anything inappropriate and even if he tried they could overpower him).
3. They tried to use car pools with people from their area.

But remember, keep your eyes open, and make sure you never hitchhike from the same place and at the same time.

Now you have a fair idea of what I mean about being aware and alert about your environment (Code Yellow everywhere). These rules pretty much apply to every situation, whether it is going from or to your workplace, waiting for your transport, or getting inside a building.

Survival Rules

- Stay alert and aware
- Look around
- Assess your environment
- Identify possible threats
- Look for alternative routes

- Look for alternative exits
- Prepare yourself in advance by keeping your cell phone ready and being armed with a key, pen, nail file, or anything else you can defend yourself with
- Look around for stones, glass bottles, sticks in your area that you can use as weapons to defend yourself
- Use colour codes to prepare yourself mentally

Your House and You

Creature of Habit

Before we go on to what you can use to defend yourself, I would like to bring your attention to the disadvantages of pre-set routines. As I have said before, 67 percent of rapists are familiar with their victims. This chilling statistic comes up in many other studies as well. A perpetrator is generally somebody from your surroundings or someone who is familiar with it—someone who knows your habits, timings, and the routes you take. In a strange way, you are unknowingly making it easier for them to plan an assault by sticking to your routine day after day. At the same time, we tend to be more relaxed around people we know and less ready to defend ourselves in contrast to when you are being attacked by a stranger. I am not talking about abusive boyfriends or husbands (that is a whole different ball game altogether), but rather people we are acquainted to you in some way or another.

First, I want you to figure out if you are one of the people with a pre-set routine? If you are, I want you to start noticing and paying attention to a few pertinent points:

- Do you notice the same people every day on your route?
- Is anyone on that route paying particular attention to you?
- Do you get a feeling that someone is observing you even if you are not able to spot anyone doing so?

Do not disregard or laugh off these feelings. Many self-defense specialists encourage women to pay close attention to all these warning signs and to rely on them because on more than one occasion this 'sixth sense' has been proven true.

Change the way you go about things. Change your walking routine or change the timing if you cannot find an alternative way. I know this is easier said than done, but if it is really not possible to change anything about your routine then please do not let your guard down. Be prepared, and if attacked, do not let the person's familiarity hamper your ability to fight. Get over your initial shock, steer your emotions towards anger, and fight back so that you increase your chances of getting away unharmed.

Home Alone

We have all heard of the saying 'charity begins at home', well so does self-defense. I agree that all of us have the right to feel safe and secure in our own homes, but we cannot take that right for granted.

Assess how secure your house is. Then establish some ground rules or SOPs (standard operating procedures) to prevent or at least minimize the chances of getting attacked at home.

If you live on your own, there are a few ground rules that ought to help minimize your risk factors:
- Whenever possible keep your curtains drawn.
- Invest in good outdoor lighting, especially around your door. If you happen to live in a rented house, and your landlord is not ready to cooperate by installing additional lighting, invest in it yourself. It is for your own safety.
- Study the various approaches to your house or flat. Be aware of dark corners or suspicious looking men frequenting areas close to your house.
- In case there are bushes or high grass in front of the house, invest in trimming them regularly. An unkempt green area can be used as a good hiding ground for a perpetrator.

If your work or your social life ensures you come home late at night often enough, then incorporate a few security measures to keep yourself secure from the time you exit

your car till you are inside your home.
- If you don't have a secure parking place, try and be creative by enlisting the help of the guard of your building or a neighbour to help you park your car at night.
- Drive past your house a couple of times before stopping. Not only will you figure out where you need to park but you can also spot anyone who may be lurking around your place.
- Once you park the car, keep the car locked till you have all your possessions organized, key in hand and then get to your door and always be aware of your surroundings—that phone call you need to answer or the text you need to reply to can wait till you are inside the house.
- Most of the houses in India have bars on the windows especially on the ground floor—make sure your house has them too, and lock your windows at night.
- Get a dog. If your living space permits and you have time to take care of it, get a dog, the bigger the better. Your home's security will automatically increase and the perception of you being a 'vulnerable' target decreases drastically.

Sharing Your Flat or PG Accommodation

If you happen to share a flat with other people or living in a PG accommodation, take extra care to ensure that you are secure in your bedroom especially at night. Always use the dead bolt to secure your room and have a sort of a weapon like a pepper spray or a bat close to your bed but not too obvious to an outsider (you don't want your attacker to get a hold of it). This will give you an additional advantage for self-defense in the case of being attacked in your room.

We all have our habits regarding spare keys to our houses or flats and, trust me; most of those habits are bad ideas. Hiding your spare key outside the house or flat is potentially very dangerous. If you have no choice try never to make it a habit of hiding it in the same place everytime.

There has been an increasing number of cases of girls living on their own getting assaulted inside their own living spaces by people who were let in. These could be delivery boys, handymen, etc. Invest in a chain lock and always insist on asking for ID before letting someone into the house—most banks and companies now have a policy, at least in principle, that all representatives must carry their ID cards, but unless we ask for them, the policy as good as not being there.

People Working Inside Your House

When it comes to the help and other people who work inside your house, try as much as possible to use someone who comes with a reference. When it comes to domestic help, take the time to register your maids, cooks, and drivers with the local police station. We all blame the police and authorities for dereliction of their duty, but let's be honest, we also don't fulfill our obligations either.

Neighbours

I am sure most of you living on your own are well aware of the scrutiny and attention you undergo at the hands of your neighbours. A girl or a lady living on her own is always the topic of conversation among the local gossips—but this is not the attention that you can rely on for comfort or security, you need to provide your own by remembering simple steps and making it a habit.

On the other hand, look for neighbours who you can call for help, who can keep an eye on your home in case you spend most of your working day outside. This can be an elderly but alert woman who can be a bit nosy but keeps a track on the people who come and go. While this can be quite annoying on one hand, it is also very useful to have someone like that on your hand side who can keep an eye on your house.

Harassing Calls and the Internet

A friend of mine, after moving to Mumbai, was subject to harassment by phone calls. She had someone calling her in the middle of the night quite a few nights in a row, which of course made her quite uneasy. She was new in town, knew very few people, and wasn't sure if it was just a prank or something more serious. Being a single woman she didn't want to take any chances and asked her company's emergency room to help her with the problem. The phone calls stopped right after that.

Harassment and attacks need not always be physical. Harassing phone calls can not only ruin your peace of mind, they can also keep you up at odd hours with the phone ringing. If this happens to you, report the number immediately. Many police forces are now offering Anti Obscene Call Helplines, make use of them.

If you happen to work for a large company that has a support number, like my friend did, involve them and take help right away.

Be very careful about sharing your mobile number on social networking sites and try to keep track of who you have given your personal number and address to. If the phone calls persist in spite of all of your efforts, consider changing the number.

Virtual Security

I have been talking a lot about being aware and reducing risk in the real world, but the virtual world provides quite a few opportunities for the sexual predator if you are not careful. Social media is all pervasive in our lives; we share practically every aspect of our day-to-day lives on platforms like Facebook, Twitter, WhatsApp, and BBM status messages. Our phones and tablets have built-in GPS and many status updates and messages which inadvertently give away our location as well. Be very aware of the pitfalls of sharing any and every piece of information about yourself on social media. Do not tweet and share your plans for the evening with times and locations—you don't know who is reading that information.

Earlier this year, a well-known public figure who is a star on one of Britain's best-known soap operas tweeted how much she missed her famous footballer boyfriend as she was home alone. The result was horrific. Her house was broken into and she was the victim of an armed robbery. In my opinion, she was lucky that it was just armed robbery, because you can always replace the jewelry and money that is stolen but never your life.

Make use of all the security features that your social networking sites offer. Read the small print, spend time looking at ALL privacy options, and click the relevant check boxes to control your personal information to the maximum extent possible. At the end of the day, you will have to take responsibility to protect yourself both in real life and the virtual world.

Meeting for the First Time and Dating

Making New Friends

The other feature of social sites is that it makes meeting new people so much easier and it is possible to feel that you are become quite close to someone through the virtual world and many people wish to extend their friendship into the real world as well. While there is nothing wrong with this in principle, you need to exercise extra caution when meeting someone for the first time.

Before getting all enthusiastic about meeting someone for the first time you need to think dispassionately and realistically.

- How well do you actually know the person you are going to meet?
- Do you have any mutual friends?

- If so, how many of those do you know personally in real life?
- And out of those whom you know in person, how many can you actually call and ask for a reference about the person you are going to meet?
- Can you trust their judgment call?

If there are no or very few overlaps between you and the person you are going to meet, I need you to stop and think twice before meeting him. Keep in mind that the virtual world is exactly that—virtual—and you can portray yourself any way you want to, and it doesn't necessarily need to be true.

Also keep in mind that there are many people pretending to be someone they are not and whose sole purpose is to lure unassuming, naïve victims. These people spend time gaining their victim's trust only to assault them the first chance they get. If you still wish to meet him you need to be very careful. Here are some rules and guidelines to remember:

- Meet in a public place you are familiar with. This gives you environmental advantage.
- If for some reason if you do not want to be seen in a place you go to often, then try to meet in a mall but not too late at night. This is a good area to meet as there are many people around and very few things can go wrong.
- Do not take any drinks unless you have seen them being poured in front of you. You buy the coffee or wait in line with him if he suggests buying it. Better suspicious than drugged!

- Try to have your best friend sitting somewhere next to you in the café or close by. Inform at least one more person about your whereabouts.
- Have an emergency SMS composed in advance with your location and the person you are with.
- Do not let him drop you off after your date! This is a very frequent mistake that girls make. A date turns out to be great fun and then he offers a ride home and girl happily accepts, only to be taken to a secluded area and assaulted by one or more attackers. Some of the most notorious serial killers, including the rapist Ted Bundy, have been known to be extremely charming and good looking. This was one of the main reason why Ted Bundy was able to get away with it for so long before getting caught. Keep your guard up. On the other hand, even if your date behaves properly the first time, do you really want him to know exactly where you live so early on in your friendship? I think not.
- Never meet in your apartment or a house no matter what you have been told! A girl usually gets invited to a 'great party' and the girl thinks it is a safe way to meet a person for the first time, only to find herself to be the only one invited along with a bunch of guys.

Dating and Parties

More and more often we hear of the term 'date rape'. What happens is that a boy and a girl go out on date where the boy puts drugs into her drink (spiked drink) and rapes her while she is passed out, unable to object or give a consent. This is called non-consensual rape. Force is not necessarily needed to complete this kind of rape as the victim is asleep or passed out while being raped.

Another common scenario is going to a party, having fun, consuming too much alcohol, and being assaulted while under the influence. Be very careful where and whom you drink with. You need to determine the people who you trust and who you can let your hair down with.

If you are at a party with people you don't know, be very careful regarding the amount of alcohol you consume and where the drinks are coming from. If there is bunch of you going out, decide on who will be 'guardian' of you all, something like a designated driver. That person will not have anything to drink and will look after the rest of you and be able to take necessary steps in case of need. Take turns when giving responsibilities and take them seriously. This way you can have fun (but it still doesn't mean you should get completely drunk) and stay safe at the same time.

- When at a party never drink out of the glass you haven't seen a drink being made in.
- Do not accept drinks from people you don't know.
- Do not resume drinking out of the same glass if you leave it unattended. Better to sound fussy or spend a bit more money than ending up with drug-laced drinks.
- Keep an eye on your friends as well. If you see some of

your friends go missing, go and find them. You may be preventing an assault.
- Be aware of your surroundings and the people around you—you may be able to see if someone is giving you attention you may not want.
- Arrive with your friends and leave with them even if you really would like to stay. If you don't know people who are staying behind, do not stay alone with them either.
- Call a cab to take you home rather than someone you just met.
- When leaving a party check if someone is following you. Remember that alcohol will impair your judging abilities as well as your abilities to defend yourself successfully. Some statistics have shown that almost one half of ALL sexual assaults have happened while the victim was intoxicated and where alcohol had been consumed either by the perpetrator or by the victim or by both. According to University of Sciences (http://www.usciences.edu/shac/counseling/daterape.shtml) one in four college going women have been date raped or attempted date raped. Around 84 percent of date rape victims knew their perpetrator and 27 percent of them did not realize what happened to them was meeting a legal definition of rape. If someone drugs you, even if you don't pass out, your judgment will get affected.

The drugs used to date rape are:
- gamma-hydroxybutyrate (GHB) and gamma-butyrolactone (GBL)
- tranquilisers, most often benzodiazepines, including valium and rohypnol
- ketamine

Being depressants, these drugs work by slowing down the nervous system, affecting memory, and dulling instincts and responses. All of this will affect your behaviour so much so that you will not be yourself and someone can easily take advantage of you. It usually takes around 20 minutes for a drug to take effect and the extent and severity of symptoms will vary depending on your size, age, and the amount consumed.

Symptoms of these drugs are:
- drowsiness or light-headedness
- blurred vision
- nausea and vomiting
- difficulty concentrating
- lowered inhibitions
- difficulty speaking or slurring speech
- difficulty in moving and loss of balance
- sensation like you are floating or loss of bodily sensation
- difficulty remembering parts of the evening or 'black-out' of events
- hallucinations
- loss of conciseness

I can relate to this as I was once served a spiked drink by someone I knew. He was a friend of a school friend of mine and we knew each other casually. At our prom night, a bunch of us wanted to continue parting and this guy had offered his house as a party place, which we happily accepted. Ten of us went for it and we had a great time until he invited me to help him out with something and to have a chat. I wasn't particularly enthusiastic but didn't want to appear rude to our host so I went. We were sitting in the kitchen and he went to pour a drink, which took a really long time to do. I even joked about why it took him so long to pour one glass of Cola. He laughed it off and said that this was a special drink for a special person, which I took as a compliment, although I still thought it was a bit weird. It was the last Cola so I offered to share it with him, which he refused on the pretext that it wouldn't be a gentlemanly of him. I insisted, refusing to drink it alone, so he very reluctantly took a few sips but maintained that I drink the last sip. I remember thinking how very weird it was but I never imagined that anyone, let alone someone I knew, would even think about spiking my drink. Soon after, I started feeling listless, as if my body wasn't quite mine, and I had trouble thinking clearly and couldn't move. I was almost an observer of this entire situation and it was like I was looking at myself from above. The conversation with the guy was still happening and it was the most ordinary conversation ever.

At that time, I had never had any drugs or cigarettes

and perhaps had a total of two glasses of wine upon the insistence of my parents. All of a sudden the conversation took a totally different turn and became more direct, regarding men–women relationships, dating, etc. I was having trouble speaking but was trying my best to behave as though everything was normal. I had also never had a boyfriend, never kissed a guy, and was rather inexperienced in all things related to a relationship and intimate contact with boys. As a matter of fact, I was quite shy, and this was the first in my life that I was sitting alone with a boy in a room. All of the sudden, he tried to kiss me and I objected and resisted, but gave up due to his insistence. It felt as if I had no will of my own, and even though I was saying '*This is not a right thing to do and that I do not want this*', my body wasn't moving or fighting back. I felt that I had lost control. He tried to touch me. I was completely confused, as this was not something I wanted or should have been doing and yet, I had absolutely no will to fight or argue or be assertive. I have no idea how long this lasted—it could have been a few minutes or a few hours. Luckily for me, two of my friends who were there with me in the same house came looking for me and insisted that we all go home as it was getting late.

I still thank my stars that they came when they did. I can barely remember walking home. I just know that I kept feeling as if I was in a dream. The next morning when I woke up my first thought was: '*What a strange dream*'. But the horrifying realization came once I saw my party clothes on the chair next to my bed. I remembered the night before and felt terribly ashamed thinking about how I had kissed a guy I barely knew, let alone letting him touch me—'*What was wrong with me?*' Was I an 'easy' kind of girl? What made it worse was when I heard rumours about him bragging that he had sex with me, which he did not, but had my friends not come I could easily see that happening as well. That made my shame even worse. As a result, I stayed away completely from all social circles and focused on my studies and sports. Needless to say, I never uttered a word about this to anyone about this. A few years later, a friend of mine came to me and just said one thing: '*That night, it was not your fault, he spiked your drink.*' I felt relieved as it all made sense. Unfortunately, nobody would give me back the two years I spent blaming myself.

You have to learn from this!

If you start noticing any of the symptoms/signs I have mentioned or if you suspect that someone has tampered with your drink, or if the situation you are in just appears weird, you have to react! React right away! Find a friend, tell them you are not feeling right, and leave the place. If you go through a similar experience which may end as rape, talk to someone, get help, and report it.

Therefore, it is very important to be extra cautious and vigilant when it comes to your own safety, as well as your mental well-being.

Waiting

There is a one more thing you need to be aware of regardless of wether you live alone or with your family or friends, and that is when you are waiting for someone to pick you up. It is always better if your friends come to your house instead of you waiting for them on the street. A friend of mine was almost kidnapped while waiting on a busy street for her friends to pick her up as it was too much of a hassle for them to drive into the colony. She spent not more than five to ten minutes waiting (it was still daytime). A few men, pretending to be policemen, came up to her and asked her to step inside the vehicle. As she got closer to their SUV she asked him for his ID and just then they got a hold of her and tried to pull her into the car. Luckily, her friends were right behind and they got out of the car and asked what was going on. The men in the car carried on the charade and tried to convince them that they had to take her. Her friends insisted on seeing their ID and also told them that they would call the police to double check. The men in the car let her go, but they started following their vehicle.

At that point she called me and asked what they should do because they were all quite scared. My advice to her was to stop at a police barricade and complain to a police officer that the men in the car behind were trying to force her into their car and were now following them. They managed to find a police barricade and the police took over from there. The SUV was stopped and my friend got away. One thing they didn't do, although I wish they had, was to file a report, because if a person can impersonate a police officer and try to pull a girl into a car in the middle of a busy street in broad daylight he is absolutely capable of doing much worse. Needless to say my friend never waited on the street again and became much more aware of recognizing danger and took a few self-defense classes as well.

In case you find yourself in a similar situation, here are a few things that you can do differently:
- If you are waiting on the street (for friends or a bus) and someone stops to talk to you to ask for direction or offers you a ride, immediately switch from Code Yellow to Code Orange as that can be a specific threat.
- Asses if there are other people in the car (if yes, then definitely Code Orange).
- Do not get too close to the vehicle. Ask him to speak

louder (it's better that he stays in the car rather than getting out).
- If he claims to be a police officer or a public servant ask for documents. Whatever you do, do not get close to the car.
- Ask him for his rank and his name and say that you will call the police to verify his identity.
- Your voice should be assertive and firm. This is to establish boundaries and the fact that you are not an easy target.
- Are there other people around you? Make a strategic move towards a more crowded place.
- Your phone should already be in your hand (as we talked about before) with your finger discretely on your ICE contact or GPS-based app (more information in appendix).
- If you sense danger, pretend to answer a call while actually dialing your ICE and give specific location details, describing the people and the vehicle in front of you. Give as much information as you can. Use some of the code words you preset with your ICE contact.
- If they start advancing towards you and/or try to pull you into the car switch to Code Red immediately (this is a trigger) and try everything to prevent being pulled into the car!
- The moment you get away REPORT the incident with as many details as possible.

Get Involved!

As you can see throughout this book I keep urging you to report incidents. No matter what happens to you or how lucky you get, you should always file a report or at least complain about the incident. Don't stop at that—talk about it, tweet about it, put it on social media, warn other women who may be going to the same area. If you do not wish to divulge that something happened to you personally just say: 'this is dangerous area' or that something unpleasant had happened to a friend of yours in that area. It is your choice how you present it, but talk about it, so that other women can be warned.

Start support groups in your neighborhood. Make sure the security guards are doing their jobs and not slacking. Vigilance is the key.

Take this one step further and report the things that don't affect you directly. For example, if you see a bus with curtains drawn or even a bus or car with tinted glasses (in most cities in India tinted/opaque glasses on vehicles is illegal), note down the registration number and file a complaint.

If you see a girl being harassed or groped in a bus or a train, make a noise about it, take her side, shout at the man, and get the people around you to help. Don't wait for someone else to do the right thing, and don't think it is none of your business. Don't be a bystander—MAKE IT YOUR BUSINESS! You never know when the situation might be reversed.

In case you see a girl or a woman being harassed on the street, act according to the situation. If there are one or two attackers, perhaps you can get physically involved and that may force them to run away. If you suspect they are armed, or think they are much stronger, you should first think of your own safety. Keep a safe distance and act from there. Call the police or a helpline. See if there is someone around to help you, make a video, or take photos of the incident. All of this can help identify the perpetrators more successfully.

Most women think that they are completely helpless or they can't do much and that it is best to stay far away rather than getting involved as it will keep them safe and away from trouble. The truth could not be further from this. If we as women start taking active interest in everything around us, keep our eyes and ears open, act and react and complain about all security irregularities and lapses, we alone can create a change and force relevant institutions and companies we work for to take action and improve our workplaces, our streets, and our overall security.

The reality is that one person's voice can easily get lost in the crowd, but if hundreds, thousands, ten thousands of us join our hands, we become the crowd, a big one. If we all start watching each other's back, helping each other, getting involved and proactive and demanding better security, it WILL result in positive change and better security. This will have another equally important impact—it will send a very strong message to the perpetrators that they can no longer get away with it because all of us are watching.

How to Get Involved

1. Report
- Never let serious incidents that have happened to you, or that you have knowledge of, go unreported.
- Keep an eye out for vehicles with irregularities: tinted/opaque glass, drawn curtains, or private buses picking up passengers.
- If a bus driver/company charter cab driver does not display their ID/credentials.
- If any driver or security personnel appears to be under the influence, refuse to get into the vehicle and report the incident to the people in charge.
- Extend this beyond your workplace to malls, cinemas, parking lots, parks, etc.
- Demand regular check-ups of CCTV cameras in your

neighbourhood. If there aren't any, see how they can be installed.
- Demand well-lit streets and report if lights are broken or not working.
- Talk to your RWA if groups of young men are using public areas in your neighbourhood to gather and drink after dark.
- Voice out your opinion if any of your colleagues in your office or college are making any sexist comments about you or any of your colleagues. This gets the message out that you are not okay with their attitude. If they do not stop, report them. As an employee or a student you have absolutely the same rights as your male counterparts, and nobody has the right to make you uncomfortable.
- If your boss or your professor is making inappropriate overtures, you should clearly state your discomfort, and if they do not stop: definitely report it. It would be a good idea to try and record them and have solid evidence to back up your complaint.
- Whenever you see an irregularity of any sort or any incident, make a video, take photos, and send it to the police and to media. There are enough fora for 'citizen journalists' nowadays; getting media attention and possibly naming and shaming the perpetrator may help the police nab him or them more quickly.
- If you have seen an area that could be dangerous—lack of street lights, men hanging around— change direction and use an alternative route. If you see another girl going

in that direction—warn her. Inform the authorities as well.

- If you see something happening to someone, for example a girl being pulled into a car or a glimpse of a woman getting molested in the car, write down the registration number, make, model, the colour of the car and the direction it was headed in and report it immediately to the police. Also call a helpline if there is one in your city and alert the media.
- Talk to your brothers and cousins about the dangers a woman faces and try to get them to take a protective stance towards other women who get attacked or harassed on the street.
- Talk to your sisters, cousins, and aunts about sensitizing young boys in your family about safety, security, and the equality of girls.
- Pay attention to the news in your city and be aware of the problem areas and then spread the word.
- At a party, if you see a girl very drunk or passed out, get involved. Organize her transport home or to the hospital if she requires medical attention (her drink may have been spiked).
- If you see someone slipping a pill into a drink at a club or a party, warn the person for whom the drink is intended or accidentally spill the drink. Send a male friend if possible, or go with more than one person, to report the incident.

- Your security and safety comes first, so whatever you do in order to help another person should not jeopardize your own safety.
- Learn self-defense and organize regular practice sessions with your friends.
- Spread the word about self-defense efficiency and survivor's mentality.
- Teach your friends what they can use to defend themselves.

Weapons to Defend Yourself

Weapons in Your Purse

So far we have been talking about how to increase your awareness, to start looking at things from a different perspective, and how to pre-empt the situation. Is it dangerous? Could it potentially be dangerous? The next step is preparation. If it could be dangerous what are my options? Preparation has two aspects: mental and physical. Mental conditioning is the most important part of self-defense.

> Unless you condition and prepare you mind to the possibility of fighting you will not be able to defend yourself!

Physical preparation has a few aspects to it:
- learning how to use things available to you
- learning self-defense moves
- and improving your physical fitness.

Let us first look at the contents of our bags. There are many things in your purse that can be used as weapons to defend yourself. In case this statement surprises you, let us go through the contents of a typical hand bag to make my point clear.

I am sure most of you carry a pen. The nib or point of a pen can be very successfully used as a knife with which you can stab your attacker, and it can be easily concealed in your hand. Look for all the things in your bag that have a sharp edge, that are relatively hard, and arouse no suspicion—you are most likely to find keys or a comb with a thin handle. Did you find anything else? A metal nail file can be a potentially dangerous weapon. Most of us carry a bottle of perfume or an aerosol spray as well. Perfumes usually come in thick and heavy glass bottles and can be useful in two ways:
- you can use it as a pepper spray—just spray the contents into the eyes of the attacker (but watch out for the wind direction, you don't want it to end up in your eyes).
- you can use the bottle to hit the attacker in the nose or anywhere on the head.

The rule of thumb is that anything with a point should be aimed at soft tissues such as the eyes, neck, stomach as this can create the most damage and everything that is dull and has some weight (you can even use your laptop) should be used against hard tissues like the skull, nose, and knees as that is where it is going to hurt the most.

I am sure I got a few raised eyebrows after the last few sentences. Let me remind you, if you find yourself in a dangerous situation where someone is going to assault, perhaps rape and even possibly kill you, I think we are past niceties and our main aim is to stay alive and not necessarily play fair—your attacker is certainly not going to.

The other useful thing in your handbag which makes a very effective and unassuming weapon is your cell phone charger. It can used as a whip (trust me if you hit someone with that rubberized wire it is going to hurt). It also, if swung around, can keep the attacker at a safe distance. And with a bit of practice, it can be used around the neck as a choker (so can your duppata).

This brings me to your clothes and hair accessories. Many things we wear can be used to help us get away. For example, a long, steel hair needle (the one we use to tie hair into a bun), can be a very neat and dangerous self-defense tool. Wearing high heels can help you get away by stamping on the foot of the attacker, while shoes with thick soles can be used to scrape against the side of the shin bone. These are just a few examples of how to use ordinary things from your handbags to defend yourself. Last but not the least, some handbags can be used as a defending tool also.

In case you haven't found anything useful in your purse, it is high time you add a few of these things. Here are few ideas about what to get.

- **Keychains**: Look for a keychain that can double up as a sharp-edged weapon. They are also known as Kobutan, and come in many sizes, shapes, and colours.
- **Torchlights**: If your job or lifestyle includes coming and going when it is dark outside, you should have a little flashlight (torch); it may not be large for practical reasons but it can help you see. If it is powerful enough it can temporarily blind or at least surprise your attacker and give you a few precious seconds to react or escape.
- **Whistles**: An ordinary whistle is very light, small, but can be very loud and used to raise an alarm.
- **Pepper spray**: Pepper spray is made from chilli powder among other things. They are easily available and affordable. They irritate the eyes to a point of temporarily incapacitating your attacker as he will not be able to see.
- **Taser guns**: In many countries, a Taser or stun gun is a popular choice. A stun gun/Tasers have a high voltage device that send an electric charge, anywhere from 20,000 volts to 60,000 volts, through the attacker's body, knocking him out for upto 30 minutes. They also come with a spring-loaded charge, which means you can stop the attacker some distance away from you because usually one of the biggest drawbacks of a stun gun is

that you have to be able to reach out and touch your attacker to use the device. Having said all of that, they are not cheap and are illegal in many countries where only police forces are allowed to use them.
- **Others:** Other things you may choose to carry in your handbag include a pen knife, screw driver, or a gun. It is important to say that any of the so called lethal weapons require prolonged training and proficiency in handling them as well as the mindset that if you take it out you have to be ready to use it. Also you will require a license for possessing and carrying a gun.

Weapon Around You

In addition to this, there are many things from your environment that can be picked up and used to defend yourself like a stone, brick, and shards of glass. Even dust can be used and thrown into the eyes of the attacker. If you are carrying groceries, you can use cans or bottles.

If you are in a closed room, look for a fire extinguisher, dustbin, broom, a hammer or pretty much anything that you can throw at, hit, or scratch your attacker with. The idea behind carrying things with which you can defend yourself is that you feel somewhat in charge of the situation and it can surprise the attacker and give you an opening to escape. None of us will carry a potential weapon and randomly attack people. However, if someone tries to attack you, you should be one step ahead of them with the situation assessed and a plan already formed in your head before the fight or flight response takes over and potentially paralyzes you and stops you from thinking and acting.

The Most Powerful Weapon

All said and done, even if you have all the possible self-defense tools in your purse, they won't help you unless you take them out and are ready to use them. I always carry way too many things in my purse, and as a matter of fact my handbag is so heavy that it can be used as a weapon in its own right. Before I came to India, I used to live alone, drive a car, and get home quite late at night. By this time the parking lot behind my building would be full and I would have to park my car in the most inconvenient place and then walk the entire distance to the building in darkness. To make matters worse, I would rarely have my keys ready and would end up spending a few minutes in front of the locked building doors searching for my key. As safety of women became a prominent topic, I started reading more on the subject and started taking self-defense classes to give myself an additional edge in dealing with a dangerous situation if it ever again arose. Soon enough, I realized that I was quite an easy target before because of the way I handled things. From thereon I never leave the car without taking my key out and preparing and unlocking the pepper spray. I figured that no attacker will stop their attack to allow me the time to look for my pepper spray.

Having your potential weapon handy and ready is only half of the process. To be able to use it and use it effectively you need quite a bit of training. First and foremost, you need to train and condition your brain. In my self-defense classes, my Sensei told me that my brain and my mind are my most powerful weapons and that the first step of self-defense starts in the mind itself. This statement is very profound and it has many layers to it. Training and conditioning your brain towards the possibility of getting physically assaulted brings a certain level of calmness and ability to think and react rationally. You can then assess a situation properly as your mind has already pre-empted it. It also gives you a certain amount of confidence.

So what to do if you find yourself face to face with someone who wants to attack you? Take a deep breath, calm yourself down, and quickly assess the situation you are in. Check if you can discretely call or send a SOS message—it is a very good idea to have any of the helpline numbers on your speed dial or make use of some of the smartphone apps that can help raise an alarm and alert people about your location. Next, try and see if you can discretely arm yourself. All of this has to be done carefully and quietly at this stage as you do not want to make your attacker even more aggressive. Once this stage is over, the time to be discreet has passed, you should be shouting and pushing off the person.

Defusing and Shifting

Perpetrators are looking for weak and easily submissive victims. If you give the impression of a confident and strong person it may catch them off guard and you may be able to run away. Pushing him off (if he's closer than desirable), saying **NO** and **STOP** are setting boundaries. The voice should be assertive and loud and words such as *sorry, please, can you, could you*, etc. have to be avoided.

No smiling either! Most women try to be polite and smile when the feel uncomfortable. You don't want to send any mixed signals. You are presenting yourself as a resolute, strong, and unintimidated person. Your facial expression and body language should portray that as well. If there are any bystanders, yell for help and tell them that you are being attacked. Sometimes bystanders are reluctant to get involved as they do not know the context of a situation. Shout and ask them to call the police. While doing all of this, do not lose sight of the fact that you are doing all of this to primarily find a way to escape.

At the same time watch your attacker's responses to your reaction and if shouting is creating a counter effect and your attacker becomes more aggressive rather than being intimidated change your tactic (as it happened in my case). Reason with him, tell him about the consequences of his actions—that he does not want to ruin his life by the spending the rest of it in jail. Question his religious beliefs, play on the fear of God, and remind him of his karma. Play on his superstition—put a curse on him and his family. Ask him if he has a daughter or a sister, and how he would feel if they were in your shoes. Be graphic. Ask him how his parents will feel when he gets caught, what they will feel when everybody hears what he has done, how his family would suffer from the stigma of having a rapist as a relative and that he has the power to change that.

You don't know what will make your attacker tick. You don't know his family values or situation, his religious beliefs, and current state of mind. You may assume this is not who he usually is and you don't know what pushed him into his actions. Therefore, before you get to the physical part of the attack try to use every single thing that comes to your mind that can make your attacker hesitate or get your attacker thinking about the implications of his intentions. This in a way is like walking through a minefield as you can as easily aggravate him more or pacify him. Therefore, you have to keep a very close eye on his reactions and keep on changing tactics if they are not working. I am reminding you that you are using all of this to create an opening for you to either strike and get away or just to get away.

There is one more thing I would like to bring your attention to while you are doing all of this—observe your attacker carefully, look for any marks on his body, his height, weight, colour of the eyes, face features, tattoos, etc. as all of this will be required when you file a case to identify and catch the person.

If talking does not work then it is time to brace yourself

and get ready to fight. The way you act and react is completely up to you. You will take your decision on how to proceed depending on your assessment of the situation as well as your gut feeling. There are no guarantees that all of these approaches and strategies will work every time and in every situation. As a matter of fact, you may think of something completely different which will be appropriate at that point of time. You may decide that talking or convincing your attacker to back off is just a waste of your precious time and that the quicker you fight back the better your chances are of escaping. Some studies show that shifting quickly from talking to striking increases chances of escape.

Once you decide to strike, the preferred way to go about this is to take him by surprise and attack first, which is a very good tactic as attackers rarely expect the victim to take charge and this may enable you to escape. Ideally as you strike you should aim to injure and incapacitate him as it is fair to assume he is physically stronger and faster and will be able to catch you as you try to run away. If you don't get this opportunity or if it fails it is time for some serious shouting, yelling, kicking, punching, elbowing, kneeing, scratching, eye gouging, biting, well pretty much using everything you can do and what you have been practicing. Playing fair should be as far away from your mind as possible. Your goal is to fight him, fight him hard, even if that means getting hurt in the process.

To Fight or Not to Fight

Many girls don't put up a fight not because they are unable to, but out of the fear of getting hurt—perhaps getting their nose broken, beaten up, or even killed. There is a common belief that if you fight back, your attacker will get more violent, hurt you more, and probably kill you. This is one of the biggest myths. In all honesty, there are no guarantees that by not fighting you will survive or that by fighting you will get hurt. It can go either way in both cases. The fact is this: if you fight you increase your chances of escaping. You should also ask yourself if you would feel better knowing you tried to fight regardless of the outcome or your fear prevented you from fighting back.

Many studies show that fighting back usually works. The effectiveness of forceful resistance to attempted rape has been well documented by many academic studies. An American study showed that women who pleaded with an attacker were raped 96 percent of the time, women who did nothing were raped 93 percent of the time, and 'A woman who violently resists gains a 55 percent to 86 percent chance of escaping injury all together'(Kleck & Sayles, 1990). Moreover, many studies have found that fighting back did not add significantly to the injury of the woman who got attacked. In fact, according to Kleck & Sayle (1990), Siegel (1989), as well as Marchbanks (1990), research showed that most of the injuries suffered by the women occurred before they fought, and while there was a correlation between resistance and a higher rate of injury it amounted to 3 percent. One way of looking at this is that the women who fought back did not get hurt because they fought back, but rather fought back because they got hurt. The higher rate of injuries (3 percent more than those who didn't fight) was mainly in the form of bruises, cuts, and lacerations rather than life threatening injuries and they occurred before the women fought back (Quinsey and Upfold, 1985).

Some women feel it is a better survival technique to stay quiet and not put up a fight. You do have this choice; however putting up a fight gives you a theoretical chance of escaping. Some research shows that raped women who had put up a fight heal and recover faster by comparison to those who didn't do anything.

What I am actually trying to say is that there is no right or wrong way of dealing with the situation, you may choose to fight or you may choose not to due to whatever reason. For example, a mother with two children may think of enduring the attack without fight because she believes that this is a better way for her to survive and be able to take care of her children. The reason can be anything that makes sense to you at that particular moment. But it should be YOUR decision. Whether to fight or not to fight should be something you choose to do, and not something your fear or apprehension has chosen for you. This may sound odd but it is very profound as it changes your perspective from a helpless victim to a survivor.

Remember, there is huge emotional trauma that

accompanies a sexual assault. However if I make a choice not to fight my attacker due to my own reasons and circumstances he may assault my body but he still cannot touch my inner self. Similarly, if I choose to fight him and it still doesn't end well for me, I do have the satisfaction of putting up a fight.

Code Red—Fight Time

If you choose to fight, there is a method to it. It has to be done with measure so that you do not tire yourself completely as a lot of attackers look for exactly that—an exhausted and completely helpless victim. In case you have tried to fight and you are just getting exhausted, you need to change your tactic again into preservation mode. Here you are seemingly giving up (like playing dead in the presence of bear), appearing submissive, or that you have fainted, which gives you the time to recover a bit, to let your attacker lower his guard and then when he doesn't expect it strike and attack again so that you can escape.

Survival

I've already said that playing fair does not apply to self-defense. Our main goal is to survive and avoid getting raped. So far, I've talked about all the techniques and tactics you can apply in order to avoid an attack and these were mainly verbal and mental strategies. There are still quite a few things you can do to escape your attacker before physically fighting him. During my research for this book, I read a number of blogs, books, articles, websites, and talked to many people from the field of Martial Arts, Special Forces—both Police and Military—and the two things that stood out prominently were the power of the mind and the second was to forget about playing fair and use anything and everything at your disposal.

My friend Tom, a US Marine Veteran and my Sensei, told me that the first step of self-defense starts in your mind and that usually sets in motion a particular series of events. To illustrate this he gave me an example of a situation where someone grabs you. He said that you can respond in two ways: you can get petrified by the thought of somebody having their hands on you. Or you can say to yourself: now that you have grabbed me, I know exactly where your hands are, and now I know where my knee is going to strike. Your mind is your first line of defense.

As you can see, the same situation can give two completely different responses and this indeed would create two completely different reactions as well as outcomes.

When it comes to being resourceful there is another 'far out' tactic I came across, which is to get your attacker so disgusted, to repel him so much that he gives up on the idea of even touching you. There are few ways you can go about this. Starting from passing gas and hoping the smell puts him off. Another way is urinating all over yourself or vomiting on yourself. The ultimate measure being excreting and covering yourself with your own excrement or what you might find on the street and cover your body, arms, and maybe even your face with it. You should not think twice before doing something like that as there is a very good chance that your attacker will get so repulsed that he will not even want to touch you, let alone rape you.

I can almost imagine the expression on your face right now but get over it! Nothing is gross if it is going to keep you alive and save you from being raped. Let me elaborate a little more on what survival means. Most of us associate survival with coping in a difficult situation, bad break up (think Gloria Gaynor's classic 'I Will Survive!') or something that is much more on the theoretical or the spiritual level. Survival of the fittest does not necessarily mean the strongest, it is also of the cleverest— the ones who are able to adapt to any situation are the ones who keep going forward. Survival is our primal instinct, it does not necessarily have to be pretty, or nice, or in line with social niceties. As a matter of fact, it has absolutely nothing to do with any of those sentiments. Your most fundamental right is the right to live and your primal, basic, survival instincts will keep you alive.

Soft Targets

Head and Groin, Knees and Toes, Knees and Toes.
Eyes and Ears and Mouth and Nose,
Head and Groin, Knees and Toes.

Modified Nursery Rhyme

Regardless of a man's size, shape, and fitness levels, there are quite a few places in the body that are as soft, thin, and vulnerable in everybody. They are called 'soft targets' and you don't need to be a martial arts specialist or a particularly strong person to be able to cause serious damage and incapacitate your attacker. First and foremost, you need to get your head around the idea that you are fighting for your life and using everything available to get away with the least damage to yourself. If that means poking someone's eyes out, so be it.

Eyes

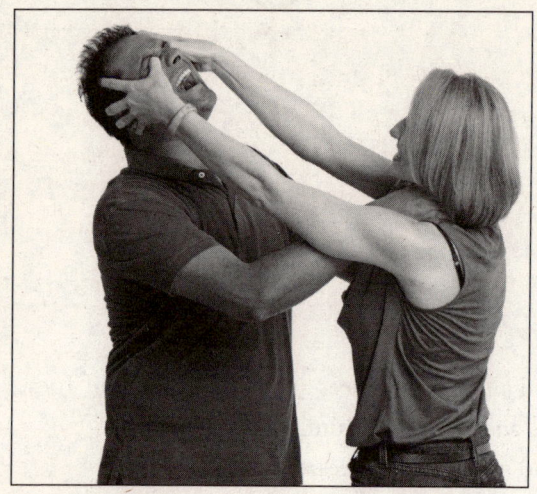

What do you suppose is common between a really strong and well built guy and a skinny nerd? Their eyes are similarly vulnerable. No matter how strong a person is, eyes are one of the most fragile parts of the human body. In a do or die situation where your survival is at stake go for the eyes of the attacker. Gouging, scratching, poking with either your fingers or with a pen or a key will give you a window of opportunity to get away from your attacker. This tactic will not only cause a lot of pain to your attacker but the temporary interference to his vision ought to incapacitate him long enough for you to get to safety.

Gouging is one of the most effective attack moves. Here we are looking at ideally digging both your thumbs into his eye sockets while the other fingers grab his ears. Think or even try this out with a tomato where you are pushing and breaking the skin of a tomato and then twisting your thumbs and pulling the skin out. You can effectively use all other fingers as well. Actually there are a number of ways how to poke the eyes and scratch the face. We will talk about it in the following chapter.

Nose

The face provides enough soft targets for you to strike in order to save yourself from a sexual attack or rape. The moment your attacker moves in close to grab you, it means clear and present danger to you but it also gives you an opportunity to defend yourself. The moment his hands are on you it also means that his face is undefended. If you have the chance, push out with the heel of your palm (see heel punch p X), ideally using your stronger hand, and strike his nose. If you can time it right you can also use your attacker's momentum against him by adding to the force of your blow. A sharp, well-aimed blow to your attacker's nose will stop him in his tracks and give you an opportunity to get away.

Head Buttting

Head butting your attacker is another excellent way of stopping him in his tracks. Your skull is very hard. A well-placed head butt not only causes a lot of damage to your

attacker, it does not hurt you as much in the bargain. This can be done in two ways: frontal or reverse head butt. In both scenarios the attacker has already entered your personal space and has his hands on you.

For the frontal head butt you are aiming to hit his nose with your forehead, either by grabbing his ears and pulling him onto you or by jumping (the way soccer players hit the ball with their forehead).

The reverse head butt can be a very effective tactic when you are attacked from the back and your attacker has his arms around you from the back. Snap your head back hard and connect with his face with the back of your head—he will not see this coming and the impact should disable him long enough to for you to get away from him. You can follow this movement by hammer hitting (see p. 98 for hammer strikes) his groin and stomping on his foot and then getting away.

If you are confident enough and have some practical experience with self-defense techniques, you can disable your attacker by first kicking him in the groin or stomach and as he doubles over force his head down further by grabbing him by the head or his ears, while bringing up your knee to connect with his face.

Ears

Eyes, ears, and the nose are closely linked to our senses; we see, hear, and smell with them. They are sensitive body parts and soft targets for you to go for when under attack. When it comes to the ears, they are better protected than the eyes and nose, but you can attack the ears as well. Most of us have had our ears twisted by our teachers, parents, or siblings bigger than us at some time or the other in our lifetime. I am sure all of you remember how painful that was. If you get the chance, remind your attacker how painful twisting someone's ear can be.

For maximum effect, try and grab both ears and twist

as hard as you can—I call it the candy wrap. Use your full hand and grab as much as of those earlobes as you can, as hard and violently as you can, and pull and twist till your attacker pulls away from you. As he is trying to get away, be careful about his counter attack. The best is to follow up this strike with another one to his knee, groin, or face. Make sure he has completely backed off before turning your back to him to make your escape.

If your attacker has grabbed you with both hands, try to slap both his ears simultaneously like banging a pair of cymbals together. Use all your might and speed. If you manage to hit your attacker hard enough or with the right timing you can inflict enough pain for him to back off and even burst an ear drum in the process.

Neck

The third possible target in the upper part of the body is the neck. It gives you a bigger target than either the eyes or the nose. It also presents enough points to attack and inflict a lot of damage even if you are not very strong. The neck has the jugular vein and the carotid artery and both make handy targets to be struck by a key, pen, Kubotan, or any sharp pointy object you may happen to have with you.

In case you were not prepared with a weapon for the attack, your bare hands can also do enough harm to your attacker's neck to help you escape. Keeping your fingers straight and firm, you can hit your attacker with a 'knife hand grip' (see p. 94) on the side of the neck.

If the opportunity presents itself, you could hurt him a bit more by jamming your elbow into the side of the neck as well. Another handy move would be to grab his Adam's Apple—a not-so-strong person would be able to choke and hurt a much stronger person by grabbing and squeezing it and pulling it out.

You can attack the neck with your hands, pens, sharp implements for your self-preservation. When confronted with a single attacker chances are that you will be able to repel an attack with a reasonable level of probability. But real life is rarely ever this neat that you get attacked when a weapon is handy. So you have two alternatives—be vigilant and a little bit paranoid and carry something sharp in your hands more often than not, or be prepared to use your hands to get to those soft targets.

Groin

A man's groin provides multiple opportunities when it comes to your self-defense. You can try kicking, kneeing, grabbing, squeezing, or scratching it. Forget about how it sounds.

Kicking your attacker in the groin is a good way to stop him in his tracks. But a lot of people make big mistakes when trying to execute this move so I am going to try and help you avoid them. When we are talking self-defense, you must always remember that real life situations take place fast and unexpectedly. You will have a split second to decide how to defend yourself, and if your initial counter attack fails it may cost you. There might not be a second chance so you have to make what you do it count. In real life, the seemingly simple groin kick if not carried out properly can injure you instead. Here are a few things to remember.

Rule Number 1: Never try a groin kick from far away! Most men expect an attack to their groin; it is almost like a subconscious early warning system that makes a lot of men turn to avoid getting kicked.

This makes it harder to deliver an effective groin kick as the attacker is more likely to turn to avoid the kick as an instinctive reaction. It stands to logic that a straight or linear kick will be effective as a straight line is the shortest and quickest way to the target. The drawback with this approach is how the body reacts to being hit in this way. When you connect with a groin kick delivered quick and straight your attacker will double up and bend forward violently and there is a high probability that you will get head butted as your momentum will carry you forward. So how do you avoid that?

You do it with a double tap. Strike high with the arm, go for a soft target in the face and then go for the groin with your knee or kick hard. By doing this, your attacker will probably not see your follow up attack and you will have an added split second to place your kick more accurately and powerfully by moving to the side of the midline. This way you will generate more power and also keep yourself out of line of the head butt that will inevitably come your way.

In case your attacker approaches you from behind, then you can attempt a reverse or donkey kick to connect your heel with his sexual organs. This may not be possible if the attacker is much taller than you, however, a very effective way is to connect with his private parts using your hips or using your hand as a hammer punch or grabbing, squeezing, and pulling the testicles with as much force as you can muster.

Fit to Fight

In the West, a lot of self-defense training teaches the 'testicle grab' as one of the main moves. The name of the move is fairly self explanatory.

You use this move when the attacker invades your personal space and you are within arm's length of your attacker. Grab the attacker's testicles (not the penis). Once you get a grip, squeeze, dig in your nails, twist and pull as hard as you can.

You can practice this grip at home by taking a pear or a small apple. Take it in your hand and crush it by pushing your nails through to break the skin and squeeze out as much juice as you can. I don't expect you to practice this with another person (trust me you will not find volunteers for this), so it is important to at least have an idea of what kind of strength is required to execute this successfully.

You don't need a lot of strength or skill for this, but what you do need is presence of mind. TURN YOUR FEAR INTO AGGRESSION. Go about it like you mean it. There is no hesitation, there are no half measures. Finish what you started (remember you are defending your life) and inflict as much damage as you can so that it gives you a precious few seconds to get away and hampers your attackers ability to chase you. On the other hand, becoming very aggressive may put your attacker on the back foot because they are always looking for a helpless and fearful target. In case your attacker is wearing tight trousers the testicle grab might not work so effectively, so punch him or knee him in the groin to get away from him.

Knees, Shins, and Feet

Knees, shins, and feet are easy targets because they are easy to strike and there is a lesser chance of you getting hurt in the bargain.

When it comes to the knees, while the front kick is better, the side kick is much safer. Whichever chance you get, aim at hitting the knee with the sole or the side of your foot, and as hard as you can. It helps if you are wearing shoes to maximize the effect of the kick.

Speaking of shoes, the next tactic would be much more effective, if the sole of your shoe is thick. In fact, the thicker,

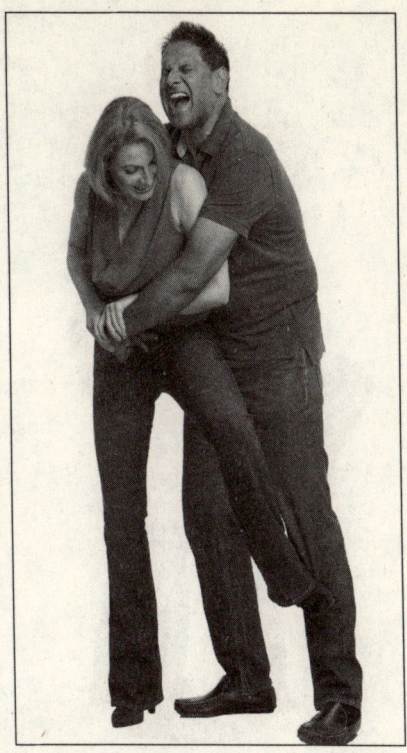

the better. If your attacker grabs you from behind or from the side and wraps his arms around you immobilizing your arms, you can try getting away from him by scraping the sole of your shoe hard against his shin. The shins are quite sensitive and it may just break his grip.

If you happen to be wearing heels (the higher and thinner the better), you can stamp your heel on his toes and drive your heel down as hard as you can on the top of his foot (this is also called instep) and twist your foot at the ankle to inflict

as much as pain and damage to the rim of the foot. Not only will he let go, there is very little chance of him being able to chase after you. I have experienced first-hand being trod on, albeit accidently by a girl who was dancing and wearing high pencil heels—needless to say it was really painful and I had to leave the party to get an X-Ray. I spent one week hobbling around with a swollen foot. Now imagine doing this with an intention of hurting someone. And of course take your high heels off when running away!

Fingers and Wrists

Fingers and wrists are probably the most vulnerable joints and this is why they represent great soft targets. On the other hand, this is also where most perpetrators grab you—by your wrist of by the clothes on your upper body.

If he is holding you by your wrist, your primary aim should be to break the grip. You can do this by attacking the weakest point of his grip which is the place where index finger and thumb meet. You simply need to rotate your wrist in such way that the thumb side of your forearm is at the weakest point of his grip and then just pull your arm out. You can follow this up by grabbing him and try to end up either breaking his finger or a wrist.

If he grabs you from behind, one of the easiest techniques you can use is the 'finger lock'. You just need to hold his fingers and pull them away and in the opposite direction to the normal range of motion. This will be quite painful and he is likely to let you go at least temporarily, which you can use to follow up the attack either by breaking his finger or punching or kicking him.

Martial Arts and Self-defence Techniques

So, what is the best self-defense technique? How to choose from so many disciplines available? There has always been a huge debate regarding this particular issue. Until recently it was commonly accepted that you just need to pick any martial arts form and it will teach you all you need to know about defending yourself. This is not entirely true.

Martial arts will not necessarily prepare you for the reality of a violent street fight, where you have a very determined attacker who does not play by the rules and where the circumstances and environment are everything but controlled. The other downside of martial art forms is that they are very precise and need to 'flow' in order to be successful and this usually takes a really long time to master. In a way this is why they are called 'Marital Arts' and not

'Martial Fighting' as they give you exactly that—an art of movement with many rules and regulations and they do not necessarily teach you how to fight.

Having said that, there are many good and useful things in martial arts. They will teach you discipline of a movement as well as how to look at an opponent from the point of strengths and weaknesses and how to (at least in theory) use his weaknesses and imbalances to your advantage.

Here are a few factors you need to keep in mind about self-defence techniques:
1. Time needed to learn it (the quicker the better)
2. Complexity (simple solutions preferable)
3. Physical strength requirements (how strong you need to be to apply it successfully)
4. 'Retaining' the information (does the technique require vigorous ongoing training?)

Krav Maga

In my researches, Krav Maga kept turning up as the most comprehensive technique that one can learn for self-defense. It was designed to teach you how to survive in an uncontrolled environment where no rules apply and there are weapons involved. It focuses on a no-holds-barred 'get your adversary down and out' approach for the purpose of street survival. No quarter is expected or given, and everything goes and is allowed if it helps you survive. Its development is credited to Imi Lichtenfeld, who led the defense of the Jewish Quarter from attacks by Fascist gangs in Slovakia in the 1930s. It is often referred to as Israel's national martial art form as it was popularized by Israel's army as their preferred close combat self-defense method.

It draws inspiration and takes elements from an adapted Wing Chun move called 'bursting', as well as from karate, Greco-Roman Wrestling, Brazilian Jiu-Jitsu, boxing (Western), and Jiu-Jitsu. Bursting is a simultaneous defense/attack—instead of blocking an attack and then delivering a response, you block the attack and deliver a response at the same time. So in reality you block with the left arm and push forward with the legs, striking the right fist to the throat—and all of this happens simultaneously.

Attacks to vulnerable body parts are encouraged. In defending yourself, one looks to inflicting testicular ruptures. Equally significant is the importance placed on disarming attackers and turning these weapons on the attacker. But most importantly it helps defense become second nature and does not require thought by relentlessly training hand-eye coordination. Krav Maga can be learnt by just about anyone in only three to six months, regardless of athletic prowess.

Keysi Fighting Method

It is said art reflects real life and this is amply demonstrated by many action movies that use real fighting techniques to create 'unreal' fighting sequences. If you have seen the last three *Batman* movies then you have already been introduced to the Keysi Fighting Method. This technique was developed by Justo Dieguez and Andy Norman, based on Justo's experiences. This technique helps you train to defend against an attack by many people. But a big drawback is that unlike Krav Maga it takes a very long time to learn. However, if you persist in learning it, you can become a self-defense machine.

The Keysi Method virtually does not employ any kind of kicks. It is about extreme close-quarter combat using every weapon the body can quickly wield in a small space. Fists, head, knees, especially the elbows are the main weapons.

Interestingly, the technique employs basically one stance: 'thinking man'—with the hands clasped on the head and the elbows raised to protect the head, neck, and upper chest. It looks like a man holding his head while deep in thought and it is very easy to learn.

In this method, instead of straight punches one uses hammer fists and sharp elbows to deliver more damage than straight punches. This is because you have to employ the entire upper body in bringing the firm, outside muscle, from the root of the little finger to the wrist, down like a hammer against the target.

The Keysi method also grew out of an amalgamation of different fighting styles. Trapping techniques are taken from Jeet Kune Do, centerline defense from Wing Chun, grappling and throws from Jiu-Jitsu and Aikido, and ground fighting from Brazilian Jiu-Jitsu. As this method teaches its practitioners to defend themselves against any number of attackers, it is a useful to discipline to follow given the ever increasing tendency of women being attacked by 'gangs' or 'packs' of predatory men. It teaches you to use a 360-degree range of aggression, and to observe all objects in the vicinity for their potential as weapons and use them as such.

Brazilian Jiu-Jitsu

Some of the most effective fighting methods to successfully defend yourself are drawn from more than one of the 'pure' fighting techniques. This particular hybrid mixes Jiu-Jitsu's standing throws and strikes with ground fighting. Ground fighting pays attention to joint manipulation and overall control of the opponent. The objective is to effectively end a fight very quickly. It also works on the premise that the larger the attacker, the more easily he can be grappled off his feet by using his center of gravity against him and forcing him to submit (or pass out).

Once on the ground, the first thing Brazilian Jiu-Jitsu teaches you is to seize an arm or a leg and to break it at the joint. This is done by using 'kneebars' for snapping knees or ankles, 'armbars' for breaking elbows and wrists, chokeholds and the use of the powerful legs to immobilize the attacker's torso and to end the fight with fists or elbows to the face.

Western Boxing

I don't want you to get intimidated by talking too much about exotic fighting techniques popularized by Hollywood as the only means to learn self-defense. One of the most effective, easy to learn and quite inexpensive fighting technique is boxing. Thanks to the exploits of Mary Kom we know that girls can learn boxing too. Boxers throw punches faster, harder, and more accurately than any other trained fighter on the planet.

Learning to box is relatively simple but time consuming. This is because boxers train for an average of four years to do just that: punch properly. They are not allowed to kick, so their hands are all they have. One of the biggest advantages in just using your hands with your feet firmly planted is that it is very difficult to get you off of your feet and knocked to the ground. The other thing about boxing is that you need to practice regularly (daily) and keep strengthening your body to build endurance and durability.

The main mantra that a boxing coach teaches his or her pupils is: 'Always protect yourself'. Your target is the side of the chin, which will wrench the attacker's head sideways and shut off his brain by pinching the spinal cord in the neck. His strength and rage do not matter. He will black out instantaneously.

Kung Fu

One of the most common misconceptions about Kung Fu is that it refers to one specific discipline. Kung Fu is actually a number of fighting styles under a common name. These styles were developed by Chinese monks in the Shaolin Temple over the centuries in their quest for better physical health and search for enlightenment. Kung Fu has quite a few 'families' and 'schools'. The art uses legends, Chinese philosophy, and mimickery of animals to make the system more effective and powerful. There are a few styles that focus on life energy qi (ki or chi) and its manipulation called *internal* and some that concentrate on improving muscle and cardiovascular fitness known as *external*. All of these martial arts techniques are divided into four areas: kicking, striking, throwing, and grappling. Then, there are throwing, seizing, and locking the joints. The important thing is that all forms of Kung Fu have all these aspects, which makes it a great self-defense technique.

There are over 400 subtypes of Kung Fu. They can broadly be divided into northern and southern styles. The northern styles emphasize the importance on kicks and wide stances and the southern styles on the utilization of the hands and narrower stances.

Here are some or the most popular styles.

Northern:
- Shaolin

- Long Fist
- Eagle Claw
- Monkey Style

Southern
- Wing Chun
- Hung Gar
- Choy Li Fut

Jeet Kune Do

The most famous martial artists of them all, the amazing Bruce Lee, developed a system which he called 'a style without style'. This may sound contradictory, but there is a sense to what he was trying to convey. He said, 'The worst thing you can do is to anticipate the outcome of a fight. You ought not to be thinking of anything but his attack and your response. Clear all other thoughts from your head, or they will slow you down.' Throughout this book, I keep saying that you must be clear in your mind as to what you have to do, to train your brain to be able to assess and re-assess situations, and keep changing tactics if need be with one aim and one aim only—self-preservation.

This fighting style also uses one stance, the Western fencing 'en garde' stance. One crucial element of this style is that you don't aim kicks higher than the waist (this cuts out the possibility of your attacker grabbing you by your foot and throwing you to the ground). This also gives you enough soft targets to aim at. The style also emulates elements of Wing Chun and includes close-quarter trapping of hands and feet. The key to Jeet Kune Do is the importance placed on the speed of strike combinations, and if you train hard and diligently you can strike the attacker's throat upto 10 times in a second.

Jiu-Jitsu

You must have noticed that a lot of the other hybrid styles were inspired from Jiu. This is because it is perhaps the most universal style on this list. Not only is it a true hybrid style that draws upon elements of grappling, hard striking, eye gouging, choke holds, biting, joint locks, it also enhances the awareness of the defender's centre of gravity versus the attacker's centre of gravity.

In this technique, you learn to bring down your attacker by lowering your centre of gravity under his and jerking him over you or around you. It's simple and effective but like anything else it requires training and strength. If he attacks with a weapon, you trap his arm and then deliver a knife-hand strike to his collarbone, while shoving him backwards and down, locking the wrist which holds the weapon and breaking it. I know it is easier said than done, but given the size disparity between your attacker and you it is very important to learn some of these techniques.

If he charges forward and grabs your top or kurta, you do not move backward. You move forward and bend down, ram your hip into his midsection, grab one of his shoulders with one hand and with the other, grab him around his back, and whip him over your own shoulder, shoving upward with both legs. Jiu-Jitsu teaches and enables a 45-kg girl to do this very easily to a 100-kg man. You can then trap one of his arms and lock one of its joints while he is down.

Wing Chun

It is said that Bruce Lee developed Jeet Kune Do from Wing Chun Kung Fu—the martial art he was originally trained in—because he rebelled against it for being too slow and formal for self-defense. That's quite misleading. The truth is that it was insufficient for him when fighting against professional martial arts experts. But when it comes to defending yourself against a single person, Wing Chun on its own can be quite adequate.

Wing Chun's signature punches do not use the hips, but are instead very fast, rapid-fire left–right punches to the attacker's chest. They are not aimed at the belly or the throat, but the sternum or solar plexus. You block the opponent's attack with one hand and respond with the other fist straight into his chest, following with the other fist, again and again, walking into the attacker as you punch. The forward motion of your whole body adds power, which, coupled with the arm strength of the average woman, results in about three times the force that she can usually generate. The only thing is to practice your speed in doing this. Sometimes one can manage fifteen punches before the attacker can react. These punches have to be dealt keeping the elbows close to the sides, which prevents the attacker from grabbing the punching arm.

If you have the advantage of becoming a proper practitioner of this technique you could then employ the centerline defense versus looping attacks, which is a roundhouse kick. The shortest distance between two points is a straight line, so instead of picking up extra power by swinging around and twisting the hips, you block the attacker's strike and simultaneously throw a front kick straight into his belly. This will take almost anyone off his feet of the first time, if you kick as hard as possible.

A shorter person (like a woman against a larger man) can benefit from the close range of this method. The closer the two people are, the easier it is for the shorter person to invade the reach of the larger person, effectively penetrating his defense.

Aikido

What I like best about Aikido is the basic underlying principle that when an attacker strikes, he leaves some part of his defense vulnerable. If you, the defender, do not attack him, you remain defensively invulnerable. It certainly does not mean that you do not resist his attack. On the other hand, you use the momentum of the attacker against him. You may or may not be a fan of Steven Seagal (he is probably the most famous Aikido practitioner in the Western world and happens to be a genuine 7th degree black belt in Aikido) but I suggest you watch his signature move the *Kote Gaeshi* or 'Forearm Return'. The move is absolutely essential to any self-defense arsenal. The attacker steps forward and throws a straight punch. You sidestep, catch hold of his wrist and twist around in time with his punch. Do it right, and it will fling him completely off balance, using his own momentum, while you whirl around and twist his wrist toward the outside. You are most likely to break his wrist. The best part is that it's actually a very easy move to learn and perfect.

Another plus point for Aikido is that the fighting style works on joint locks, which do not require much speed to perform, and are extremely effective in immobilizing and incapacitating an attacker. The downside of Aikido is that it is all about timing. If your timing is not perfect, not only you will not be able to execute the move properly, you will probably end up right in the line of the movement and can get thrown off your balance or hit hard. It requires a lot of practice and over a period of time also becomes a meditative process about the flow of movement and power of momentum.

Karate

When we usually think of martial arts, Kung Fu and Karate are probably the first two names that come to one's mind.

There are also very commonly mixed up. So it would be remiss for me not to mention both. In my opinion, Karate definitely has some merit as a self-defense fighting style because the focus is on deflecting the attack.

In real life, a majority of punches or knife lunges are performed straight at you and not in an arc. In order to counter this, step to the side, creating a lateral line toward the attacker's arm, strike the attacker's punch or knife hand, and then quickly strike his lower side, belly or back with your other fist. This is very difficult to defend against, and he will most likely not be able to. Push forward and throw a knee into his quadriceps. This hurts like crazy.

Hitting the face and head are important, but to surprise your attacker punch him with your other hand straight into the soft spot below his sternum as hard as possible, twisting the hips. Target his solar plexus to incapacitate him. It is as effective as striking the groin. If you don't think you are strong enough then snap a front kick straight up with the ball of the foot planted as hard as possible into his groin.

Kick-boxing

It is easy to look at theoretical scenarios, but the fact is that it is far more likely that if you're on the street and a stranger attempts to mug you or worse, he most likely doesn't know any particular fighting style. While survival and street fighting are inherently ugly it helps to know a particular fighting style or technique to help you instill some discipline and allow you practice. Kick-boxing is as good an option as any of the others I've mentioned, and probably more easily accessible than some of the other fighting techniques.

Kick-boxing as a self-defense form is excellent as it is aimed at all available openings and relies on punches, knees, and kicks. It is fast-paced, distracting, and unless the attacker has a knife or gun, the defender has more of an advantage as she is armed with more weapons—hands, feet, knees, elbows, and head.

I have mentioned this before that very often a lot of girls fail to fight back for the fear of injury even if they have a chance. If you take up kick-boxing under a teacher you will have to undergo something called 'combat qi', which is the physical conditioning of any part of the body through repeated damage, until it no longer sends sufficient pain signals to the brain to bother you. Simply put, you will be hit on your shins and elbows with sticks repeatedly till you get used to the pain. If you can overcome your fear of getting hurt, there is a great chance that you will overpower your attacker. Kick-boxers will roll a smooth stick up and down the shin firmly enough to cause pain for about an hour a day for two years. The tibia is repeatedly damaged and rebuilds itself stronger and thicker. Eventually, a kick-boxer can kick a baseball bat in half with his or her shin and not feel any pain.

Kick-boxing will teach you coordination between your hands and feet, to punch and kick in combination. All of this will come in handy when defending yourself if you end up being attacked and are left with no option but to fight.

Basic Self-defense Moves Everyone Should Know

The aim of this book is to help you prepare mentally as well as physically to save yourself when you are being attacked. In the next two chapters we will talk about basic hand positions, punches, and kicks, as well as how to break out of some of the most common grips. We will also go through the fitness routine which will help you strengthen your body physically. Being fit plays a significant role in the amount of damage you can do with your punches and kicks as well as the amount of time you will be able to fight without getting too drained and exhausted.

As we can never truly predict every possible scenario I will present you with the most common grips, holds, and situations to give you an idea as to how to go about a similar situation. However, you have to make the decisions depending on your circumstances.

So, what to do when you have exhausted all other possibilities? Fight or not fight? The choice is yours. If you choose not to fight it should be your choice due to the circumstances you are in and not because of fear. However, if you choose to fight you have to go all out! Turn into an animal that is pushed into a corner and is doing everything to survive. Everything is allowed and the game is not played fair. You will do everything and anything to survive. Strike hard and strike fast. Use everything to your advantage— gouging his eyes, scratching, taking the skin off his face, or biting him.

Biting, as primitive as it may sound, is a very good self-defense survival technique. Here force is of the essence. Wherever you decide to bite it should be wide and as hard as you can. Imagine a lioness taking down her pray and biting the neck of a gazelle. That lioness should be you. Neck, face, or even an arm are all good choices for a powerful bite. Ideally they should be followed by an additional attack to the face, body, or groin. Use everything you have to survive and remember, every possibility your attacker provides you with is a possibility to escape. Here I literally mean anything! For example, if he forces you to perform fellatio (oral sex) on him, BITE IT OFF! The moment his penis is in your mouth clench your teeth as much as you can and pull your head to the side. The pain will be so excruciating that he may pass out, giving you an opportunity to run away. The same can be applied if his testicles are anywhere near your face.

Repeat after me: 'I will survive and I will stay alive and I will do anything to stay alive!' That is a survivor's instinct.

Usually all of this comes a bit later. In the beginning, as your attacker invades your private space, the first thing you need to do is to get loud and push him off.

Get Loud and Push

As soon as your attacker touches you or if you are cornered, shout as loudly as you can. It could be 'Back Off or 'Don't Touch Me' in any language you are comfortable with and push him back as hard as you can. What you can hope to achieve with this are either of these things. It conveys to your attacker that you are not a victim or a pushover and it is a call for help too. This may work but will probably not repel all attackers. However, it certainly causes predators that are looking for easy targets to back off and leave you alone.

Open-handed Strikes

Open-handed strikes cover different techniques where you strike your attacker with your hand without making a closed fist. The best known of these techniques is the Karate Chop also known as the Knife Hand strike. You use the edge of the hand closest to the little finger or use the opposite edge of the hand—this will also protect your thumb from possible injury. It is often delivered by bringing the arm down in an arc halfway between the horizontal and the vertical plane to your attacker's forearm or neck.

You can use the same technique with the palm facing towards the ground and strike the attacker in the throat aiming for the Adam's apple or for the attacker's eyes. This is called 'Nukite'.

One of the greatest advantages of an open-handed strike is the ability to quickly grab the opponent to perform a follow-up, such as a throw or a pull into another strike. The extra control this affords when compared to a punch is worth the larger risk of damage to the hand or fingers.

Ridge Hand

Ridge Hand or Reverse Knife Hand is made by tucking the thumb into the palm of your hand and extending a few centimeters along the inside of the hand just beneath the knuckle of the index finger.

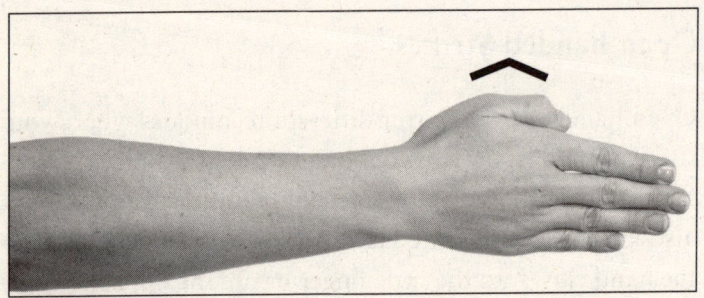

You can deliver a blow with this technique in a straight line or by bringing down your arm in an arc depending on the target. You can cause injury to your attacker's side of the neck, nose, jaw, eyes, and you can even try to go for the groin. But be careful, if you miss your intended target, this can hurt you as well. So practice the technique well against suitably hard targets in order to get used to it rather than being forced to use it for the first time in a pressurized situation.

Any self-defense technique is as good as your ability to use it; this depends on not only your physical fitness but also your expertise. Pick up a few moves you think you might be comfortable with and then you have to practice, practice, and then practice some more!

Spear Hand

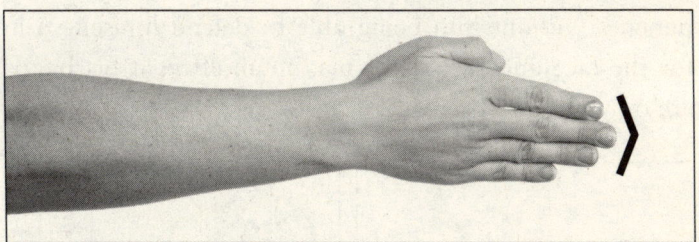

The Spear Hand is yet another useful technique that you can adopt. With the Spear Hand you hit your attacker in the same way as the straight punch, the difference being that your hand is held open like the Knife Hand or the Karate Chop.

Just a word of caution, as you will be leading and hitting with your fingers pick your target (soft target) carefully, otherwise you might break one or two fingers. On the other hand, the advantage of this technique is that it adds a few inches to your reach. Go for the eyes or the throat to make a strike with this technique count if you get attacked.

Straight Punch

A straight punch is thrown in a straight line from your shoulder to the attacker. Throw the punch ideally with your stronger arm, but you can punch either with your left or your right arm. As a straight line is the shortest distance between two points a straight punch is the quickest way to hit someone. If the attacker is already onto you and you are inside his defensive line you may be able to deliver straight punches without him being able to defend himself. Aim for the face and throat for maximum effect if his hands are on you.

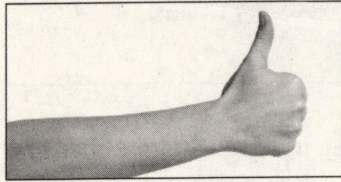
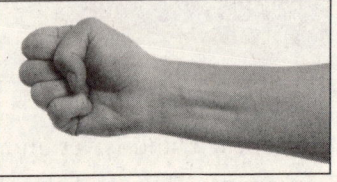

Before you punch take care to make a fist properly. An improperly made fist will end up hurting you more than inflicting any kind of damage on your attacker. Roll your fingers tightly so that there's no space. Seal your thumb tightly over your fingers near the first knuckle. Never cover your thumb with your fingers, it automatically loosens the fist. If your nails are long, you might find it difficult or uncomfortable to make a fist. You have two options: cut your nails or opt for open-handed strikes.

With a straight punch you are going to use your knuckles to strike your attacker. Generate power from the ground by softening your knees, using the energy in your legs, engaging your core, and extending your arm fast and hard by rotating your hip and shoulder. Take care to keep your elbow down and your wrist straight to deliver the punch with maximum force and to minimize the risk of injury to yourself.

In case his hands are aiming higher then you should aim lower—go for the solar plexus or for his groin, and the moment he drops his hands to protect himself from your attack go for the face.

Instead of punching straight with you parallel to the ground, bend forward a little so as to drop your body down and make use of your legs to generate more power. Aim for the stomach, just above the belly button, and lower down for the groin region. Never try to punch down leaving your head up as it may allow your attacker to hit you in the face before you connect. Make yourself as small a target as you possibly can, and bring your punching hand back in front of your face as soon as you can in order to get your guard back up.

Heel Punch

Punching by using your knuckles can mean that you may bruise or injure your knuckles after a few strikes. If that is the case you can try a variation called the heel punch. I would advise girls with long nails to use this as the first alternative. The area to strike with is the base of the heel of the hand just above the point where the top of the wrist meets the hand. Do not use the entire hand as the force of the punch will not be as concentrated. The basic technique stays the same as the straight punch but target the chin, jaw, throat, nose, or the side and back of the head.

Hammer Strikes

Hammer strikes make use of the bottom of the fist, the side with your little finger as opposed to your knuckles. It provides protection for your thumb and can deliver devastating blows to the chin, nose, and jaw of the attacker. Hand is raised up to the eyebrow level, and once you deliver the blow bring the hand back into a defensive position.

Hammer Fist Downward Punch

There are variations of this technique that you can use against your attacker with devastating effect depending on the body part you are targeting. The downward punch is

very effective against the back of the head or the neck of the attacker if you manage to get behind him. In case you manage to get your attacker down on the ground, a well placed downward hammer fist punch to the face should keep him down long enough for you to escape.

Like the basic hammer fist, make a fist and raise your hand and as your fist comes down, rotate your shoulder and hip inward and forward and drop your weight at your knees to generate maximum power. Avoid bending at the waist to prevent disturbing your balance to deliver the maximum force possible. Get as close as you can to your attacker (take a little step forward if necessary) to be perfectly stable as you deliver the blow.

Hammer Fist Punch to the Side

Use this to hurt your attacker's chin, jaw, nose, or the side of neck. If you get attacked, get into neutral position, keeping your feet hip width apart, hands by your side, weight evenly balanced between the two feet that will allow you to shift your weight at a moment's notice. Tuck in your chin, get your shoulders up, allowing your elbow to lead the motion so that you are still secure defensively. Lift your hand sideways with your elbow bent, make a fist, rotate your hip and shoulder outward while the leading foot turns a bit the other way. Once you are attacked, face your attacker—you need to be aware of what he might do to counter your defense. Lead with the outside foot and bring the fist down, leading with the side of the hand with the little finger as hard as you can against your attacker.

Elbow Strikes

Many self-defense experts emphasize again and again the thumb rule—'Strike soft targets with hard surfaces and hard targets with soft surfaces', i.e. the nose or throat with your elbow and the heel of your palm to strike the back of the head. Your elbow is one of the hardest parts of your body and you need to use it as much as you can in case you are attacked.

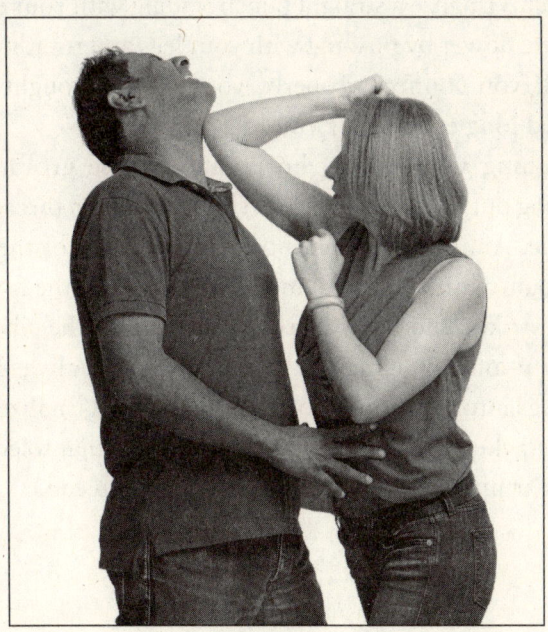

Like hammer fist punches, you can deliver an elbow strike at a few angles. They are particularly effectively in close quarters and make a very effective weapon in defending yourself when your attacker invades your personal space or is already in contact with you. Lead with the tip or the edge of the elbow, focus all your power and strength in a small area, bend your elbow, and lash out.

As the human elbow can move in many directions, let us explore how that can be a handy weapon in your defense against an attacker.

An elbow strike along the horizontal plane is usually struck in front, aimed at the face or the throat of the attacker. Visualize a straight punch leading with your elbow; generate power by pushing with your legs and rotating your hips. If you connect properly, your attacker ought to be stunned long enough for you to get to safety.

Keeping your elbow horizontal to the ground but swinging out sideways will help you neutralize a threat from the side. Aim for the chin, nose, and the side of the head or throat to inflict maximum damage. As with the forward elbow strike, lead with the edge or the tip of the elbow by raising it and swinging out and sideways, as always push your legs into the ground to generate power. Visualize what your attacker intended to do to you and use that to convert your fear into rage and strike as hard as you can.

Fit to Fight

That versatile elbow of yours is also a potent weapon if you get attacked from behind. If you get grabbed from the back, tuck in your chin to prevent your attacker from choking you, bring your shoulder up to give your elbow the freedom to move, turn your hip, pivot with your outside foot (remember the technique for the hammer fist punch), use the foot on the inside to generate your power to swing that elbow to incapacitate your attacker. Bring that elbow down and back in a vertical plane to slam into the sternum or stomach of your attacker to get free. If the attacker is a lot taller than you, then you can always try and pull him down by the wrist and swing your elbow upwards to connect with his throat.

Kicks

When fighting hand-to-hand, you have to use whatever you have at your disposal, and you cannot ignore the longest limbs—your legs. Punches, elbow strikes, and hammer strike punches are most effective when the attacker invades *your personal space*. On the other hand, if you are trying to hit your attacker who stays just outside the reach of your arms or to drive him back once you create an opening with a punch, then kicks are your best option.

The rising kick to the groin where you connect with the upper shin works best in close quarters, or if you connect with the instep, you can strike from a little distance away. In most cases, our legs are the strongest limbs and if used properly they can be used to inflict maximum damage to your attacker while staying at a safe distance from him in order to get away.

I think it is also time to remind you of another basic philosophical principle of self-defense—**remove yourself from danger the first chance you get.** The object of using these techniques is first and foremost to remove the threat and get away from danger, and that should never be forgotten.

Knee Strike

Like the elbows our knees can be used to inflict maximum damage to your attacker in close quarters. You can target the groin, liver, kidneys, solar plexus, the face, or the head with your kneecap and the point just above the knee cap for maximum impact. Remember, whenever possible soft targets are hit with hard surfaces, but in a fight you connect with whatever and wherever you can to disable your attacker—if the situation allows you to get into the basic fighting stance.

One foot in front of the other, hands up to protect your face and head, balancing on the balls of your feet. Take hold of the attacker's upper arm just above the elbow with

your left hand. Now with your right hand, grab his neck or right shoulder trying to grip as much as you can, and hit him in the neck with your right forearm. Pull his body down towards the ground and at the same time bring your knee up by rotating and pushing through your right hip, aiming to connect with your kneecap. From here, you can aim either for the groin or his solar plexus. Regain solid footing quickly so that you don't give your attacker any chance of grabbing it in case he is still on his feet.

Offensive and Defensive Front Kicks

With an offensive front kick you can try and hurt your attacker anywhere from the area around the bellybutton down to the groin. You are aiming to connect with the ball of your foot.

Bring your knee up to the chest with the toes of your foot arching back towards you, push or 'punch' your leg out straight, smashing into your attacker with the ball of your right foot.

The defensive variant of the front kick, unlike the offensive front kick, is to push your attacker back, giving you some room to manoeuver to fend off the attack. You have to use the entire sole of your foot so that the object of the kick is not penetration, unlike the offensive front kick, but to push him back using maximum thrust.

If you find yourself backed up against a wall or a car, use the opportunity to plant a defensive kick and give yourself space from your attacker. The effectiveness of this technique depends on timing more than anything. If you kick out too soon there is a danger of injuring your knee, and if you kick too late you might not connect properly and fall away when you make contact.

If you are trying to kick and hit the chest or upper torso of the attacker, you start off the same way as the offensive kick—with your knee pulled straight up to the chest, toes pulled back. But instead of completely straightening your knee on impact, keep the knee slightly bent as you hit your opponent. If you are able to swivel your hip using the obstruction that you are pinned against, you should be able to generate enough power and with the right timing you should be able to push your attacker back with the sole of your foot and launch your counter attack to be able to disable your attacker.

Round Kick

A variant of the front kick is the round kick where instead of the kick being delivered straight it is delivered along the horizontal plane. Use it to strike against your attacker's leg or ribs. If you manage to pull your attacker's head down either by grabbing him by his hair or ears, you can always target his head with the round kick as well. Connect with the shin or the instep of the foot.

Start off as if you mean to use the front kick but instead of pulling the knee up to the chest, swivel your hip while rotating quickly on the foot planted on the ground and kick through with your leg in a horizontal arc. Keep your knee slightly bent as you make contact with your attacker as it will keep your knee from hyper extending (overstretching). Immediately, the same way as with the all other kicking techniques, regain your base by bringing your kicking foot back to stabilize and protect yourself as soon as possible.

Note:
- Rotating outwards on your stabilizing foot is vital to generate maximum power to be able to deliver an effective round kick. You want to rotate or pivot

on the ball of your foot so that you are able to move and shift your weight from one foot to the other smoothly and quickly and this will also enable your heel to move out to strike the attacker.
- The round kick need not be delivered in a horizontal arc, it can be delivered at any angle and the angle depends on what target your attacker is presenting you with. Assess the situation, look for an opening and deliver the kick. Remember real life situations are messy and unpredictable and you will never find textbook situations to deal with. You have to turn your fear into rage or anger and use that aggression to do whatever it takes to stop your attacker and for you to get away to a safe place.

Front Kick to the Upper Body

Most self-defense experts will always advise their students to aim low with their kicks. This is also a safer practice as you don't expose your body to too much counter-attack. Your centre of gravity stays low and you are more stable. The front kick to the upper body is executed in the same way as the front kick to the groin, and you can use this if and when your attacker doubles over and is not standing tall. You aim is to hit the face or the torso and try to connect with the ball of the foot.

Lift your right hip and move forward and follow in with your knee slightly bent. As you rotate your hip forward, flex your toes and lead with the ball of your foot and extend your lower leg violently to connect with the head or upper body of the attacker. This kick is and can be a follow up to a counter strike to the upper body or if you manage to grab the attacker by his ears, neck or shoulders and pull his lead low, or as a follow up to the front kick or rising kick to the groin. As always, read the situation—if it makes sense to connect with the instep or the shin, change the contact point; what matters the most is that you connect and disable your attacker rather than the technique.

Rising Kick to the Groin

This is the variation of the front kick where we are aiming to connect with the groin area of the potential rapist and stop him in his tracks. Trust me, if you connect correctly there will be both pain-related and physiological impediments for him and he won't be able to attack you.

The main difference with the rising front kick and this variant is that you are aiming to ideally connect with the instep or shin, but the technique stays by and large the same. Remember to rotate the heel of your base foot inwards so that you are able to swivel your hips to generate maximum torque and inflict maximum damage. If possible, remember to keep your hands up to protect your face, and try not to kick too high. If you are able to do so, kick him more than once to ensure he is unable to either further attack you or follow you as you get away from danger.

Short Uppercut Back Kick

If your attacker grabs you from behind there are a couple of techniques that you can deploy with your feet and legs to break his hold. If your attacker is substantially bigger than you and if you get grabbed in a bear hug and lifted off your feet, you can use the short uppercut back kick to try and break his hold.

Imagine you are trying to kick your own backside with your heel. Bend your knee sharply and try and connect your heel with his groin. It will help to lift up the hip of the leg which is still on the ground to give you more power for the kick.

Downward Stomping Kick

Wearing heels can make this technique a devastating self-defense move, and it will work best if you are wearing footwear other than slippers or Kohlapuris. Even then with the right amount of rage and sense of self-preservation you can use this technique against your attacker. You can aim at your attacker's instep (the top of the foot), ankle, and in case you have managed to get your attacker on the ground, a well-aimed downward stomping kick to the head or the groin is going to keep him on the ground long enough for you to get away. You hit with the bottom of your heel. Like I said, heels help in maximizing the effectiveness of this kick.

Bring your knee up to the chest; flex your toes to ensure

that you lead with your heel. In order to safeguard your knee, try and keep it slightly bent as you connect with your attacker, not only will you reduce chances of injury but you will also maximize the force you generate.

Side Kick

The thing that a lot of self-defense instructors do not like about martial arts is that they are too structured, 'too clean' to deal with real life situations. You are never going to be so lucky that your attacker will allow you to take up the right defensive position before attacking you. An attacker can come at you from any side and more often than not they will try and attack you from behind or from the side. The most effective self-defense techniques equip you with a 360° sense of awareness of danger and how to deal with it.

If the attacker comes at you from the side, you can use a side kick against him. You lead with your heel, and aim for the stomach or solar plexus or you aim below for the knee. You lead with the leg closest to your attacker, swivel your hips in the same direction as the attacker, lift your knee and foot up in front of your body and strike out with the heel. Rotate the heel of your foot that is rooted to the ground so that the heel is pointing towards your attacker. Try and connect with the bottom of the heel, and keep the knee slightly bent at the time of impact.

Note: Bend your body over the hip away from the attacker to generate more power and to aim higher. Use this kick for an attacker who is on the side but someone out of the range of your arms.

Kicks When on the Ground

When we visualize a fight we often forget to be realistic. While it is important that you visualize a 'how to fight scenario' and keep it realistic, it is very possible that your attacker will knock you to the ground and that you will not be in a position to execute any of the kicks or strikes you may have practiced from an upright position. If you do get knocked to the ground, it is very important not to panic. You still have enough opportunity to strike back. If your attacker stays upright you can aim for the knee, or in case he bends down to come close or tries to position himself on top of you, he will leave himself vulnerable to a kick while lying down.

When on the ground, you can use two basic positions to kick from: lying on your side or lying on your back. They both have their merits and demerits. You will be a bit more mobile when on your side, and when you are on your back, your head and face stays away from the attacker.

You can practice kicks from the side by lying on one forearm, hip, and the leg below all on one side. Use your hand that is away from the ground to protect your face.

Pull the knee of the leg that is higher to the chest and be ready to kick. In a real life situation, take a call once you are knocked to the ground whether it is possible or feasible for you to take one or the other position while on the ground. The one thing you must always do is pull the knee of the leg on top close to you, keep an eye on the attacker and be ready to strike, position or no position.

Back Position

Lie flat on your back and then lift your shoulders and head off the ground. Tuck in your chin so that it rests on your chest, your hands stay free and up to protect your face, bend one leg and push it into the ground to give yourself a base, the other leg is pulled up, ready to strike out.

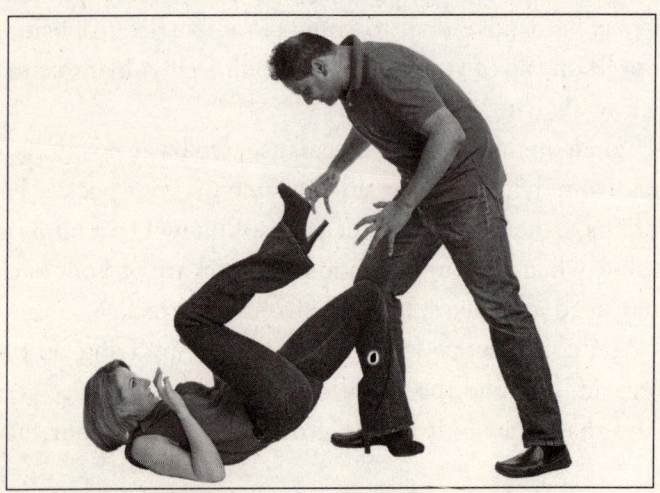

Front Kick from the Ground

Use this kick if you are on your back on the ground. It can be very effective if the attacker stays directly in front of you. Aim for the head, throat, or chest if he is on his knees and leaning into you, otherwise aim for the groin or shin if he is standing over you.

Use the bottom of the heel or the whole of your sole to strike. Push your leg firmly placed on the ground to generate more power. Your core plays an important part in this to maintain your balance. Pull the knee to the chest and imagine you are stamping down had you been standing up. As soon as you make contact, immediately bring the knee back to a bent position over your body, ready to stomp again.

Another variation of this kick is if the attacker is already on top of you. The first thing you need to do is to bring your heels as close to your bottom as possible and then in one fast and powerful movement push your hips upward by

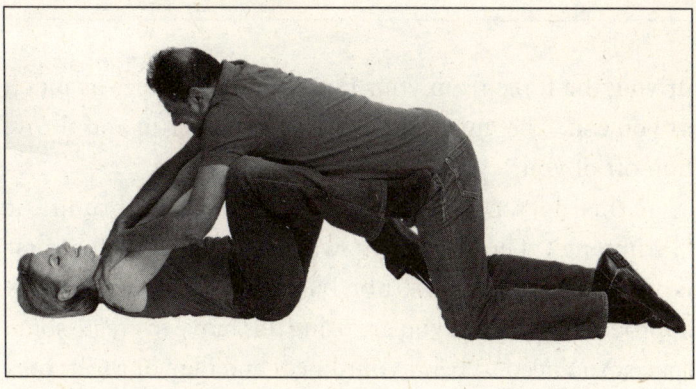

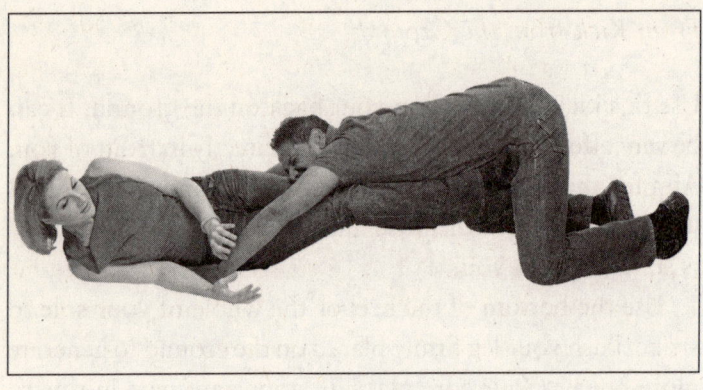

driving the force from your hips, glutes, and legs as much as you can. The impact of this can be powerful and throw him off of you.

If this does not work, you may try the 'Shrimp' or 'Shrimping'. There are two ways you can do this: first is when the attacker is not lying on top of you but is approaching you and you are using this move to create some space. You need to bend your knees and dig your feet, toes and balls of the feet into the ground and push them both as you rotate your body and lift your bottom up. Once you do this, release the position. It will get you away from your attacker onto the side of your body. From this position you can deploy the side kick to get away.

The other way is if the attacker is on top of you. In this case, you will first make a little 'side step'—just move one leg a bit more onto the side, push the heel into the ground, press the opposite shoulder blade down and push away. The leg you are pressing down will be the side your 'shrimp' goes, so if you push through your right leg you will move to the right. You can then use the free leg to place it on the attacker's hip, use it as a step, lift your hips up, and kick him hard and as many times as possible with the other leg. This of course requires a bit of practice, so get down on the floor as start practicing!

Round Kick and Side Kick from the Ground

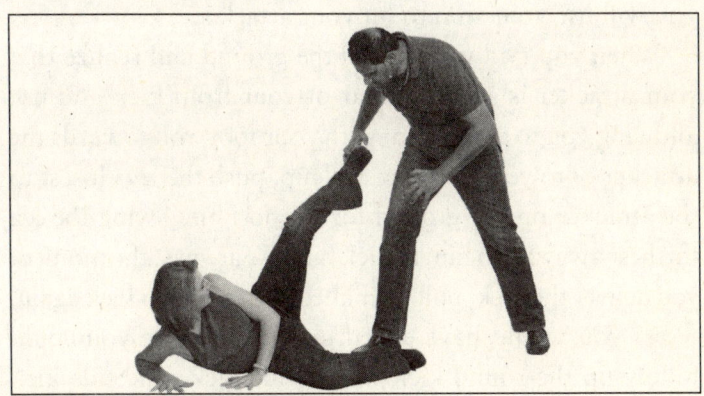

This is a good tactic to use if the attacker tried to go around your normal kicking arc, i.e. go away from your kicking leg. If this happens you can get down, roll onto your hips and employ a round kick with the leg on the other side to the attacker. You can aim for his groin, knee, and depending on how low he is perhaps even his head. Your basic starting position would be back on the ground and you will use your shin to hit your attacker.

When you find yourself on the ground and realize that your attacker is steering clear of your front kick and not allowing you to stomp him with your foot, roll towards the attacker onto your forearm and hip, push the leg closest to the attacker on the ground for support and swing the leg furthest away from him to kick him. As always, the moment you deliver the kick, pull your knee back ready to kick again.

As you would have ended up on your side you could follow up the round kick with a side kick. The side kick would target the knee, torso or the attacker's head or for that matter, any body part within easy reach of your foot and leg. Push the hand closest to the floor into it for support, extend your hip and extend your leg for power. If the attacker is staying out of arm's reach, then use both hands to support yourself and as you connect with your attacker the shoulder, hip, knee and your heel should be in one line. Pull the leg back and be ready to kick again.

Basic Defensive Movements Arms

Even if you are carrying a weapon—real or improvised in your handbag—it is going to be a very uncommon occurrence that you have it handy when you get attacked: unless you prepare yourself physically and mentally to always be on your guard. One solution would be to carry your pepper spray or Kubotan or whatever implement you have in your hand at all times when you are moving from Point A to Point B and the other is to also memorize and practice basic hand defensive positions and moves to defend yourself.

We will first see basic positions on how to target and disable your attacker's wrist.

First Position

If your attacker comes at you from the front, you can stiffen your fingers and raise your forearm high and almost

level with your forehead. Use peripheral vision rather than focusing on one point of attack. With your raised hand you will be to block an attack from the front coming down at you; attempt to meet the attacker's wrist with yours.

Second Position

Keep your arm at an angle raised around the level of forehead to protect against an attack coming at you at an angle.

Third Position

Raise both your arms pointing towards the sky or at 90° to the ground to block an attack coming from the side.

Fourth Position

Bring your elbow close to your torso and hold it tight to protect a blow to your ribs. Let your forearm extend out slightly at an angle to protect your stomach as well.

Fifth Position

Invert the second position and bend your arm at an angle to defend against a blow to the lower body.

Sixth Position

Bring your arm parallel to the floor and low in front of your torso while bending slightly at the waist to defend against a blow to the centre of the body.

When you are using your arms to block offensive blows, use the blade of the arm to take the impact. Bend at the waist not at the knees; this will give you more stability while keeping your body away from the attacker. Keep a 90° bend at the elbow, and always try and meet the wrist on wrist—this way your attacker cannot get past you easily.

Two-handed Pluck to Counter Front Choke

This is an extremely important technique that is used to free yourself if an attacker comes at you from the front. If he starts choking you need to react right away as you don't

want to faint due to lack of blood supply to your brain. There are two ways you can go about it:
- Use the two-handed pluck to extricate yourself from his hold and at the same time launch a counter strike. More often than not your hands will instinctively go to the point where your attacker has grabbed you, use this movement by creating hooks with your hands.
- Lift your hands over your attacker's arms, reach into the gap, your fingers should curve out making hooks. Be quick as you don't want to use your strength against your attacker's strength, you want to use speed and the momentum to get his hands away from their point of contact. As you get his hands away from your throat or shoulders trap the attacker's hands close to your body. This has two purposes: to delay a follow up attack from him and give you a window of opportunity to deliver a

counter attack of your own, probably in the form of a knee to the groin and to remove yourself from danger as far and quickly as possible.

The other option which probably might work even better is that when your attacker has his hands around your neck. Quickly place both your arms inside his choke and using your strength, drive upwards and outwards to make him release his hold on your neck. Follow up with a groin kick.

Choke from Behind

In most real life situations, you are most likely to be attacked when you are least expecting it. You can reduce the odds of this happening by being vigilant and properly observing your surroundings, assessing the threat of people around you. If you are taken unawares, the first and most important thing is not to panic. You can be smaller and not as strong as your attacker but even if he may be in control physically, he cannot control your thoughts and your mind is your first line of defense. So, don't panic, evaluate the situation and see what you can use in your defense.

If your attacker grabs you from behind and wraps his hands around your neck and throat you are in immediate danger of being choked due to the supply of oxygen being reduced to your brain which can result in you passing out or worse, dying. It will also throw you off balance, make you panic, and enable your attacker to knock you down to the ground. So how do you get yourself out of this hold?

Put your hands together and push them back and up hard, grabbing and pulling his wrist and thumb down. Tuck your chin so that once his hands come free of your throat he will be unable to wrap his hands around your throat again. You need to lift and round your shoulders to further protect your throat. You may try to break his finger or/and his wrist. If you are unable to break free yet, or as another option, place one hand or a few fingers underneath his choke, then step back and sideways to the side of the other hand and use your free hand to deliver an open-handed slap hard to his groin. Turn to face your attacker and then employ whatever technique that comes to mind to stop him—elbow strikes, kicks, etc. Your focus is solely on making the attacker let go of you and giving up on the idea of following/chasing you.

If you are not sure of being able to execute this move, you can stomp on his instep with your heels, scrape the sole of your shoe against his shin, and try and snap your head back to reverse head butt him. All the moves I am describing to you in this chapter are to teach you how to save your life but always delve into your primal instinct for self-preservation and do whatever it takes to get away.

Side Choke Defense

If the attacker comes at you from the side and tries to choke you, the danger is similar to when you get choked from behind. To get out of this attack use the one-handed pluck. The technique is similar to the one you use for the two-handed pluck; you make a hook with the hand further away from the attacker. When it comes to this technique, be it the one- or two-handed pluck, the accent is always on speed—you need to catch your attacker unawares and use momentum and speed to execute this successfully.

Always remember to tuck in your chin to maintain the blood supply to your brain, pin the hand of the attacker to your body and use the split second to deliver your counter attack. Spin around and deliver an open-handed slap to the groin or stay facing him and knee him repeatedly in the groin. If he falls to the ground, you can follow up with a downward kick.

Headlock from the Side

An attacker can get you into a headlock from the side by wrapping his arm around your head and neck with the intent to make you submit and immobilize you either by knocking you to the ground by restricting your blood supply to the brain or choking you.

As your arms extend out instinctively to avoid falling, turn your chin in the direction of the attacker's hands and tuck it in towards your body to prevent him from choking you. Move your outer hand towards your attacker's groin and your inside hand between your head and the attacker's head. Strike the groin either with an open slap or punch. With your inside hand, grab his face with your thumb under his chin and the index finger below the nose. Push his chin up and his head back and hit him as often as you can with the palm heel or hammer fist strikes.

When you are confronted with this kind of an attack, use the attacker's strength and let him pull you and then use that momentum against him. Always try and attack both his groin and face at the same time. At the crucial moment remember to use whatever you can. You may have practiced this technique with a friend time and time again but in real life use whatever blows you deliver should be as hard as you can—it does not have to look pretty what is important is that you get away.

How to Counter Arm Pulls and Wrist Grabs

It has been observed in many cases that the attack does not come out of the blue. Very often potential attackers either know the victim or are at least familiar with them—they know their demeanor and body language. They try and pick on a person who is perceived to be timid and least likely to fight back. If a person who is familiar with your routine and is in the habit of passing lewd comments or trying to harass you on regular basis, stop him before he decides he can get away with more. Report him, and if he crosses a line and tries to touch you, deal with him there and then.

Second Crime Scene

There have been numerous instances where a girl gets pulled into a car while waiting at a bus stop or by the road side. The perpetrator then drives away to a secluded spot and rapes the victim there. This secluded spot is called the Second Crime Scene. You need to do everything in your power not to get taken to the Second Crime Scene. If you are able to resist getting pulled into the car it stands to chance you might escape getting attacked more seriously.

Remember that in situations where you could be fighting for your life there can be no half measures, you might not get a second chance. Even a seemingly innocuous act like grabbing your wrist has to be countered with a full out counter attack. This way your hands will not be in the control of the attacker, and most importantly your attacker will quickly realize you are not a pushover and he will not bully you into submission.

Release from Wrist Grabs

If your attacker suddenly grabs your wrist in an attempt to pull you to an area you don't want to go or to immobilize one of your arms to subdue you into going with him, twist your wrist in his direction, thereby immediately weakening the grip between his thumb and forefinger. Push the elbow of the arm he has grabbed out and pull your forearm away. Immediately follow this move with

a hammer fist strike to the neck or a round kick in order to get away.

If your attacker grabs your right wrist with his right arm, i.e. reaching across, the basic technique remains the

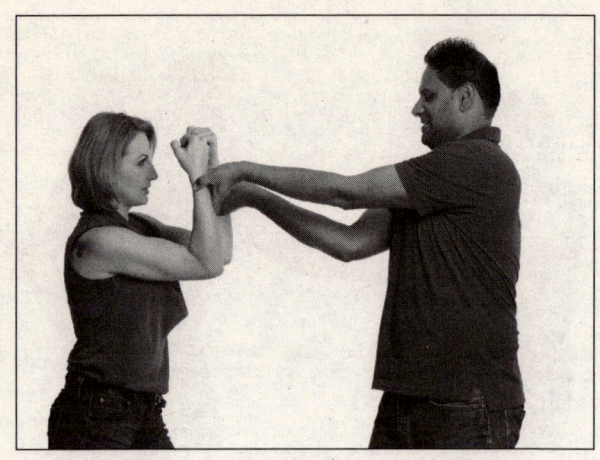

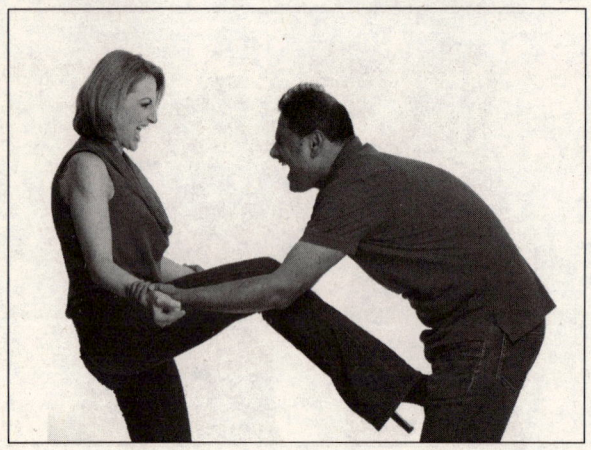

same—rotate your arm outward away from your body. Then exploit the weakness in the attacker's grip between the thumb and the forefinger and pull your arm away and immediate follow up with a strike with the other arm.

If an attacker grabs both of your wrists with his hands, bring your elbows up close to his elbow and violently pull away, then follow up with a knee to the groin. Try and rake his eyes with your nails and get as far away as you can from danger.

Fit and Strong

It sounds like a cliché, but the fitter and stronger you are the more effective your self-defense moves will be and the better your chance are of successfully escaping. What I mean by this has four aspects to it.

To begin with, you will be more capable and by extension more confident that you can actually defend yourself. Secondly, when striking back there is a greater likelihood that you will create some serious damage because of the power of your punch/kick. Thirdly, fighting is a hard task and very draining. The fitter you are, the longer you will be able to fight. Lastly, once you get the opportunity to run away you may be able to outrun your attacker. So what do we need to do in order to improve our fitness levels?

Get Active

First and foremost—get more active. This can start with something as simple and modest as going jogging which can be interspersed with walking—try to do at least 3 to 5 km per session. This can take you anywhere between 20 minutes to an hour (our normal walking speed is between 3.5 to 5 km per hour). Take the stairs, and try to walk as often as you can. All of this will help you increase your cardiovascular ability and stamina.

One of the great ways of living a healthier lifestyle is to surround yourself with like-minded people, and running groups are an excellent way to meet new people with similar habits and draw from their experience. As most groups do outdoor running, spending a bit of time exposed to the morning sun will do wonders for your bones and the exposure will help your body produce the required amount of Vitamin D that is essential for your body to absorb calcium, which makes your bones strong.

If you cannot find a running group, then organize a 'get fit for self-defense group' with your fellow students, colleagues, or neighbours. You can work on your physical fitness, as well as use this time to practice all the movements, grips, throws, punches, and strikes we have been talking about.

Another good option is to join a gym where you have the entire facility at your disposal and where you can work on not only your cardiovascular capacity but also start improving your strength with some resistance training.

Resistance Training

Working with weights is known to be the quickest way to improve your strength. Please do not fear that you will end up looking like Arnold Schwarzenegger. If it were so easy to bulk up and get chiseled, then don't you think many more men would look much more muscular than they do? For a woman to get a body like that naturally is almost impossible and would require many hours of dedicated and hard training each and every day, accompanied by a very strict and measured nutritional system. So don't be afraid of weights.

The other thing I would like you to start paying attention to is not only the way your body looks but what your body is capable of doing and understanding where your weaknesses are. So while you may be concerned about a little extra weight on your thighs (which is fine and you should take care of that), your priority should be making your arms stronger. The old saying goes: 'You are as strong as your weakest link.' So first, take care of your weak spots.

In the following programme, we will focus on the functionality of your body, which will take care of your weaknesses and in turn will give you not only a strong body, but a good looking body as well.

The following programme I have developed for you does not require any equipment and will help you condition your body regardless to your current fitness level and, if practiced regularly, will give you a powerful and strong body.

Warm Up—Inch Worm

Stand with your feet hip width apart and arms stretched all the way to the ceiling. Inhale and stretch all the way down so your hands touch the floor. Walk forwards on your arms into a push-up position—walk with your feet so that your legs go all the way up to the hands. Repeat 4 to 8 times movements. If the space does not allow you to keep moving forward, do one movement forward and one movement backward. On the last count, go into push-up position and hold for a count of 10, 20, or 30.

Inverted Letter V and Cobra

From push up position, go into the inverted letter V by lifting your bottom as much as you can to the ceiling and dropping your hips as low as possible. Do between 5 and 15 repetitions. Relax in the Little Piece of Heaven position. Repeat 2 to 3 sets.

Time Challenge

In the next sequence, do as many repetitions as you are able to in 20 seconds, followed by 10 seconds rest for beginners. Intermediate level does 30 to 45 seconds with 10 seconds rest, and Advanced level does 1 minute of each exercise with no rest in between.

The amount for sit-ups is double than for other exercises. The speed of the exercise will depend on your fitness levels. I would prefer that you focus on your posture rather than the speed of the exercise in the beginning.

1. *Overhead Squats*

Stand with the feet shoulder width apart, arms hanging next to the body. Inhale and bend the knees as much as possible ideally touching the floor with your hands. As you exhale, straighten your legs, engage the core muscles and push the arms over the head. The movement should be even and controlled without any jerks. As you get stronger, you may add dumbbells to your workout, or you can simply fill thin plastic bottles with sand and use them as weights.

2. *Push-ups*

Get into the push-up position and go as low as your strength allows you to. Make sure not to drop your hips and not to arch your lower back. If you are struggling (as most girls do) you have two options: either to hold the static position (without movement) or to go down on your knees, cross your feet and lift them off the ground into so-called 'girlie push-up' position and do your movements there. As your strength increases progress into the full push-up.

3. Reverse Lunges with Bicep Curls

Pick up your weights (or soft drink bottles), stand upright with feet hip width apart, inhale. As you exhale, step back with one leg as far back as comfortable and bend both knees. At the same time, bend both elbows into a bicep curl. Step forward, and repeat the same with the other leg.

4. Bottom Raises with Arm Up

This exercise is not as complicated or difficult as it may seem at first glance. Bend the knees and put the arm a little behind your back, inhale and push your hips up as much as you can balancing your weight on three limbs; the other arm should be up, reaching towards the ceiling. Bring your bottom down and raise the other arm to the ceiling and lift your hips up off the ground. Make sure not to stress your shoulder while executing this movement, and keep on engaging your gluteal (bottom) muscles while raising your hips.

5. Overhead Squats

Repeat the same movement as described above.

6. Side Jumps

Start from the push-up position and then jump forward with both your feet to the side of your hands. Jump back into the starting position and then jump forward with both feet to the other side of your hands.

7. *Reverse Lunges with Bicep Curls*

Repeat the same movement as described above.

8. *Crunches*

Lie flat on your back with both arms stretched over your head and inhale. As you exhale, come up into sitting position with knees bent and close to the chest. Make sure to keep your core muscles engaged and not to take the movement from the back. Remember we are doing crunches for double the time.

Once you have completed these eight exercises, rest for one minute and repeat one to two more sets.

Now that you know the exercises we are doing, here is the order in which you will do them for your plan.

1. Overhead Squats
2. Push-ups
3. Reverse Lunges with Bicep Curls
4. Hip Raises with Arm Up
5. Overhead Squats
6. Side Jumps
7. Reverse Lunges with Bicep Curls
8. Crunches (Double Time)

Level	Duration (seconds)	Rest (seconds)	Sets
Beginner	7 x 20 + 1 x 40	10	1-2
Intermediate	7 x 30 - 45 + 60 - 90	10	2-3
Advanced	7 x 60 + 1 x 120	0	3

As you will soon find out, this is quite challenging, however don't get disheartened and discouraged. You can modify the speed and pace yourself accordingly. Remember we are building a body that will help save your life.

Drills

The next set of exercises will not only strengthen and shape your body but at the same time will help you practice some of the self-defense movements.

1. Punches

Stand in a defensive position with your hands making fists and with your left leg forward. Extend the right arm forward as if you are punching. To start off, we are not moving the body too much, we are not using any weights, and we are not punching into anything (punching bag). Do 30 to 50 repetitions with your right arm, followed immediately by the same number of repetitions with the horizontal elbow strike. Bend the arm at the elbow, keep the forearm and upper arm parallel to the floor, and push your elbow as far back as it goes. Keep engaging the core throughout the exercise and add some more power to your movement by pushing the movement from the hip not only by stretching and bending the arm. Change the foot position, and repeat the same on the other side.

2. Weight Shifter

For the next two minutes, keep both arms close to the face (defensive position), and lift your feet off the ground, lightly shifting your weight from one foot to the other.

3. Combination Strike

Steady yourself with your feet parallel and stretch the right arm forward and make a movement as if you are going to reach out to grab something and pull the arm back as much as possible. Stretch the arm forward, open the hand, turn the palm down, lock the elbow, and with a straight arm stretch it back as far as possible. This movement resembles a combination of elbow strike to the back and open-handed slap to the groin. Once you are done with one side, change and repeat on the other. Repeat 30 to 50 movements, alternating between elbow and locked open-handed slap.

4. Knee to the Face

The next movement is a variation of the knee strike to the face. Imagine you are grabbing someone by the ears, tightening your core, and pulling his head down while at the same time your knee is driving upward. Once you are done with the one side, repeat the same movement on the other side. I want you to do this movement as fast as you can for two minutes (one minute each leg). Stay on the balls of your feet, and do not disengage your abdominal muscles.

Defenders

Stand with the feet hip width apart, place both arms right in front of the face, with the elbows touching each other. Your hands should be made into fists. Inhale and as you exhale open your arms straight out, then close them in front of your face again and pull them down under the angle while pushing the elbows as far back as possible. Repeat 30 to 50 times.

1. Straight Leg Kicks

For the next two minutes you are doing forward kicks one minute each leg. Place your left leg forward with your knee slightly bent and the gluteal muscles engaged. You right leg is behind and straight with both arms in defensive position. Inhale, engage the core and bring the back leg forward into a kick position. Repeat the movement with as much power and speed as comfortable. Inhale, while the leg is back, and exhale as you are kicking. Ensure the core stays engaged and that you are balancing your body on the steady leg.

2. Alternate Punches

Stand with your feet shoulder width apart and parallel, and create a movement that resembles punching alternating between right and left arm as fast and with as much force as possible. Keep on moving for a duration of one to two minutes.

3. Side Kicks

Shift the weight completely onto your left leg and lean to the left side a bit, lift your right leg as much as you can. Repeat 10 to 20 times just by lifting and lowering the right leg up and down without putting any weight on your right foot. After that, lift the right leg up and keep it there and execute the kick to the side. Bring the right foot down to the ground, get into the starting position and repeat the kick. Arms should be in front of your face throughout the movement. Shift the weight onto your right leg and repeat the same two exercises with your left leg.

4. Knee to the Chest

For the next two minutes, do the knee to the chest movement, doing one minute for each leg. The movement should be a powerful upward lifting of the knee as close to the core as you can without you losing stability and the core connection.

5. Slide Side—Squat with Pull

Stand with your feet hip width apart, lift your arms up above your head to the right. Exhale, push your left leg out to the side, bend your left knee, and simultaneously pull both your arms diagonally to the left. Inhale, bring the legs and arms together to the start position. Repeat 10 to 20 times each side.

6. Spot Running

For the next two minutes do spot running. Spot running can be done as a slow jog or a sprint or a combination of the two depending on your fitness level.

7. Lift and Reach

Next is a lifting and reaching movement. Take a cushion or a flour sack ideally weighing between 1 to 3 kg. Place it on the floor in front of your left foot and inhale. Bend your left knee, reach down and pick up the cushion bring it up to the chest, and reach up over and up to the right side diagonally from the place you have picked it up from. Bring it back down to the starting position, and repeat 10 to 30 times. Change the side and do all the steps starting from the right side.

8. Russian Twists

Start from a deep squat position with feet shoulder width apart and bottom as much to the ground as possible. Arms are up, elbows bent to 90°. Inhale and turn your right foot all the way in and bring the knee down to the ground. Change the side and repeat all of this on the other side. Ensure not to put pressure on the knee; this movement should be done from the core, quadriceps, hamstring, and gluteal muscles. Repeat 5 to 15 times on each leg.

9. Cardio Lunges with Twist

The next exercise will really get your heart rate up. If you are a beginner, you can do this exercise for 30 seconds and gradually build your way up to 2 minutes of continuous movement. Get into the lunge position with the right foot forward, left foot as far back as possible.

Dip down and turn your torso and your arms to your right side. Inhale and use your core strength and your leg strength to jump up. Change your legs and twist onto the other side. Focus more on dipping deeper than jumping higher.

10. Overhead Circles

You will need an object with some weight for this exercise. You may take a baton, a cricket bat, or if the bat is too heavy, start with a more compact weight, for example, a liter soft drink bottle filled with sand. Take it in both your hands and do a slow controlled movement very close to, but not touching, your shoulders and upper back. Repeat 10 to 30 times on each side. Ensure you don't stress your shoulders.

11. Push-up Jumps

Start with a deep squat stance with your feet wider than shoulder width apart and arms in defensive position. Inhale, put your hands flat down on the floor and jump back into push-up position while exhaling. Inhale and in one smooth movement jump forward and move your arms back to the starting position. Repeat 10 to 30 times.

12. Coordination Cross Jumps

This is a very tough exercise which is not only going to improve your coordination but will work on your upper body and core strength as well.

Put your lower body on the left side with your hands in front of you and to the right. Bend the left knee and lift your weight off the ground by using your right arm and left leg. Your right leg should be inside between your left leg and right arm; the leg is slightly off the ground as well as your left arm. Inhale and as you exhale swiftly shift your position onto the other side by shifting the weight onto the opposite arm and opposite leg. It may be slightly complicated in the beginning, but with a little bit of practice you will be able to execute it as a swift and fluid movement. Repeat 5 to 15 times on each side.

13. Push-up Lunges

Start with the deep lunge position with the right leg forward and the left leg back. Inhale and bring both hands down to the floor. As you exhale, quickly change the position of yours and lift the arms off the ground into the starting position. Repeat 5 to 15 times on each leg.

14. Charging Ape

Get into a deep squat with your hands flat on the ground and your bottom close to the floor. Inhale and use your leg muscles to propel yourself forward and lift both hands off the ground at the same time. As you land on both your hands, lift your legs off the ground to the starting position. Repeat 3 to 4 'jumps' and do the movement in reverse. This is counted as one—do 3 to 10 sets. The movement somewhat resembles a charging ape.

15. Push-up Parachute Jump

Get into push-up position, holding the body firm and still. Inhale and as you exhale drop down flat on the floor and lift both arms and legs off the ground as if you are free falling through the air right before opening the parachute. Inhale and spring up back into push-up position. Do 10 to 30 movements.

With this, we have completed our standing drills.

How to Design a Programme

If you are a beginner, your execution will be slow as you should be watching your posture and core engagement. The number of repetitions will be 5 to 15 depending on the difficulty of the movement. Remember, the more you learn how to engage the core, the more powerful the movement (the punch or kick) will be. You will have better balance, which means you will not be easily pushed off and thrown down. As your strength and proficiency improves there are few rules about progression.

Things you can change:
1. You can increase the number of repetitions per exercise.
2. You can increase the number of exercises.
3. You can add resistance—weight to the exercise.
4. You can work on speed.

This is the ideal order of progression. Having said that, whichever parameter you add on or increase, you have to decrease all the others. For example, if you started with x number of exercises and started doing them with the maximum number of repetitions and now you want to challenge yourself additionally, you can either increase the number of exercises or add some resistance. As you do that, the number of repetitions should go down as your volume of work and difficulty of execution has changed. Once you do that, you can work your way up to gradually increasing the number of repetitions.

Speed is the last variable you should work on. Logic being, if you are unable to do a movement properly slowly, trust me you will be not be able to it fast. It will just set the wrong movement pattern, and over a period of time can lead to an injury. Always change only one parameter.

Floor

The next sequence of exercises will help you improve your core strength and coordination and it will shape and strengthen your legs.

1. Hip Raises

Lie down on the floor with your knees bent and fingers interlocked behind your head. Elbows should be on the ground. If you find this position too challenging you may place your arms alongside your body. Inhale and as you exhale push your hips up as much as you can by squeezing your glutes. The movement should be powerful with loud exhalations every time you go up, and by squeezing and pushing hips as much as you can. Repeat 20 to 50 times.

2. Hip Raise Crunches

Keep your hips off the ground, interlock your fingers at the base of your head, and keep your elbows as wide as possible (you should be comfortable), and go into a crunch position without lowering your hips. For more work on your glutes, you may lift your toes off the ground. Repeat 15 to 40 crunches.

3. Opposite Arm and Opposite Leg Kicks

Bend both legs and lift the right leg off the ground. Support your head with the right hand, and reach with the left arm to the right leg. Inhale and as you exhale stretch the leg out and move the arm in the opposite direction reaching as much as possible. Repeat 15 to 30 times. Change and do the movement on the other side. Ensure not to wobble with your hips and to keep your core muscles involved.

4. Shell Crunches

Lie on your back, bring both knees to your chest, interlock the fingers on the base of your head, and bring the head as close to the knees as possible. Inhale and stretch the legs out as much as you can. Open the elbows, and as you exhale, close the elbows in, bring the knees towards the chest and heels towards the bottom. Repeat 10 to 30 times.

5. Hip Raise Kicks

Lie down flat on the back with fingers interlocked at the base of your head or alongside your body. Inhale and lift your hips off the ground, pull the right knee to the chest make sure that your hips are balanced. As you exhale, push the right leg out as if you are kicking someone. Inhale and pull the knee into the chest again. The second kick should be slightly higher than the first one. Repeat 10 to 30 times kicks alternating between low and high. Once you are done, change sides and do the same movement for the other leg.

6. Cycling Criss-Cross

Interlock the fingers at the base of your head, lift both legs off the ground, and do the first 10 cycling movements with your arms on each side. Beginners will only do this much. Intermediate and Advance level practitioners will continue with this exercise adding the arm movements making the opposite elbow reach to the opposite knee. Do 5 to 15 times for each leg. Speed should be controlled with the focus on core engagement.

7. Roll-up to Stand

Inhale, stand with your feet hip width apart, arms up towards the ceiling. As you start exhaling, go down into squat position and roll down onto the ground all the way back. Inhale and roll back up into standing position. This movement requires practice but with persistence you will be able to execute it properly. Repeat 5 to 10 times.

Side Movements

The basic position for side movements is always the same. Lower leg bent at the knee, lower arm bent at the elbow with the weight distributed between the hip and the forearm of the lower arm. If you are finding it difficult to balance your weight on your forearm and you start stressing your neck and shoulder, you may lie down on the floor with your lower arm serving as a cushion.

1. Front / Back Kicks

Get into starting position, lift your upper leg and place it parallel to the floor. Pull your knee into the chest as much as your flexibility allows you and stretch the leg forward till it gets completely straight. Ensure that the leg remains parallel to the ground. Bend the knee and pull the heel close to the bottom and in another movement, push the leg diagonally back without arching your back—this is counted as one. Ensure that leg remains parallel to the floor at all times. Kicks should be executed with control and power, and the diagonal movement should be done through the heel. Upper arm should be placed in front of the body providing additional stability. Repeat 10 to 30 times and then change the side.

2. Rotational Kicks

From the basic position, place one foot on top of the other foot. Your knee should be pointing up to the ceiling. Inhale and stretch the upper leg all the way up to the ceiling and in a one smooth movement. Lower the leg all the way until it almost touches the floor in front of you. Tighten your core even more and lift the leg back into the starting position without stressing your back. Bend the knee and repeat all the steps. This exercise should be done 10 to 30 times on each side

3. Side Kicks

From the starting position, pull the knee into the chest with the other knee slightly lower down. Inhale and connect to the core and as you exhale, push the leg slightly upwards forcefully. Repeat 10 to 30 times.

4. Side Lift-offs

Inhale and pull the upper knee into the chest. As you exhale, lift your upper body off the ground. Place the upper leg on the floor with the knee bending and pointing towards the ceiling and the heel on the ground. Rotate and stretch the opposite arm. Inhale and go back into starting position. The movement has to be done smoothly and fairly fast. Ensure that you do not stress your back while doing this exercise. Repeat 10 to 20 times on each side.

All of these exercises will work on improving your upper and lower body strength, increasing the elasticity of muscles, helping them to react quicker. They will also improve your coordination and balance and since all of these are functional movements based on self-defense, they will give you a strong and powerful body and will familiarize you with punching and kicking movements. The reason I am telling you all of this is that in real life situations there will be many factors playing a role. It is not going to be a controlled environment. You will get scared, your vision will narrow (due to the fight or flight reaction), and your body will go into fighting/executing mode where you do not have time to leisurely think things through. So the stronger you are, the more your body is familiar and prepared for the movements, and the better your chances are of effectively defending yourself. Needless to say, your mind has to be pre-conditioned before all of this.

Design Your Fitness Programme

Ideally, I would like you to be active 6 days a week. Out of which, there should be at least 3 to 5 cardio days in combination with 2 to 4 routines designed from the above given exercises. Having said that, I would still like you to have

2 days dedicated to perfecting self-defense movements, which you can organize with your friends or you can sign up for.

The Sample Routine

Day 1: Cardio 20 minutes, drills, and stretches at the end.

> **Note:** You can do all the drills in one go or do the sequence upto Russian twists as **Drill 1** and on another day do the other exercises as **Drill 2**.

Day 2: Cardio consists of walking/jogging for 30 to 40 minutes, followed by Inch Worm and Cobra routine (warm-up), post which you will do the Time Challenge and finish with the floor routine.

Day 3: Rest/movement or skill practice

Then repeat the same order for the rest of the week.

If you want to additionally challenge yourself, you can alternate between Day 1 and Day 2 without a resting day and doing your additional movement/skills practice on days 2 and 5.

What If...

There are a few more things I would like to mention which may not be our main topic, however they are very important.

Robbery

- If somebody is trying to rob you, try not to save your things because they are less valuable than your life.
- Create a little decoy and throw it away from you, this may give you an opportunity to run in the opposite direction.
- If you are with your child and someone snatches a bag from you, first ensure the child's safety and then only try to get the guy. There have been cases where thieves try to steal a mother's bag just to get her distracted from

their main target—kidnapping the child. So, here again, whatever is in that bag is less valuable than your life. Secure your child first—pick the child up and hold him/her in your arms and raise alarm, perhaps someone else can stop the robber.

Armed Attacker

- If the attacker has a gun, try and run. He has a gun and you may as well assume that he is planning on using it. Most of the killings are done from a very close range, and putting distance between yourself and the attacker means you are are increasing your chances of getting away.
- Shooting a gun and hitting a moving target requires a high level of training. It is not an easy task under any circumstances, and adrenalin, low visibility, and perhaps alcohol all play a role in lowering the precision, so running again helps.
- Run in a zig-zag line rather than straight and keep your head low as this will make it additionally difficult for him to shoot you.

Multiple Attackers

What do you do if you are in a situation with multiple attackers? I have been hearing over and over again that if you put up a fight you will get hurt more and the violence will be worse. To fight or not will be your choice depending on many factors and the circumstances under which the attack takes place, such as place of the attack, window of opportunity, etc. When you are being attacked by one or by many, you don't know whether their initial idea is to rape you and kill you or if they just want to assault you and let you go. You don't know if you are dealing with sociopaths and serial killers who get a kick out of molestation, torture, and killing their victims. You don't know if they intend to kill you after the rape so you can't report the crime.

In all honesty, it can go either way. There is enough evidence to show that women are attacked, tortured, and killed regardless of whether they resisted or not. You need to take a decision primarily based on the opportunities or windows of escape and not out of fear that they may turn more violent.

- If you have been taken to the Second Crime Scene, try everything in your power to raise an alarm before getting there.
- If you are in the car booth, try breaking the brake light and waving at people to raise alarm.
- If you are in the house, listen to the sounds around and try to raise an alarm if someone seems to be passing by.
- If you choose to fight them, it has to be done early on or whenever you see a window of opportunity, with the intention to run as far away as possible. This is a very important point. Your fight is carefully calibrated and

aimed to create or use the window of opportunity. Save your energy and when you decide to strike, go all out with all your might.
- Go for the leader. This may startle the others and give you a precious opening. The other possibility is that the followers are not as keen as the leader and the group may dissolve once the leader is gone.
- Get as many details regarding your attackers as possible.

Safety of Children

Being a mother, I feel that this book would be incomplete if we don't talk about the safety of children even if briefly so. When it comes to protecting your child, it is a combination of three things:
1. Observation
2. Inspection
3. Information/communication

1. Observation

Observe your child's reaction and look for changes in your child's behaviour. If all of a sudden, your child's mood has changed drastically don't brush it off. In case you start noticing changes in your child's behaviour don't stop there, talk to your child as well as with the child's teacher.

2. Inspection

Even if you don't notice any behavioural changes in your child, use the bathing time to discretely inspect the child's body for unusual bruises or marks that should not be there. There is nothing wrong in being extra careful when it comes to our children as none of us know when a perpetrator can strike. Sadly enough, when it comes to children, perpetrators are usually people they know. They can even be family members. This realization as painful as it is will still be less painful than letting your child go through it over a period of time just because you chose to close your eyes to the obvious.

3. Information/communication

- Talk to your child regularly and tell your child that there are no secrets between you two.
- If your child comes to you and tries to tell you something, listen and explore. In many cases, children tried to tell their parents/other adults about what was happening to them only to be told that they were lying, imagining things, and were brushed off. This would result in the child keeping it to her/himself as no one believed them anyway.
- **Circle of Trust:** Educate your child about 'safe' and 'unsafe' touches. This is something you can do with children as young as three years old. Make it a lesson. Teach your child the parts that no one apart from their

mother, sometimes father, or grandmother (you can modify the list) can touch. Parts are: breasts, bottom and parts between the legs. No one but people you specify should be allowed to touch those areas without a parent present (for example, a doctor's visit).

The next step is what should a child do if someone does touch her/him (children molestation is high both in male and female children). The child should shout and run as far away and find her/his 'safe person' (ask your child to identify her/his safe person—someone the child trusts). In turn, the identified 'safe person' will ALWAYS pay attention and won't accuse the child of lying and imagining things but will act. This is a very simple yet effective exercise that can help you build a closer relationship with your child and give your child a clear instruction of what a safe place is.

- Teach your child not to take chocolates, chips, candies, etc. from strangers as well as from people who are friendly or known to the child. The best is if the child is taught not to take anything from anyone (apart from people approved by you). If someone tries to give something to the child, he/she should tell you right away.
- Talk to your child about her/his school, teachers, and friends. Be involved and know what is happening in your child's life.
- Check the security measures in his/her school, how good and reliable their drivers and security personnel are. In case you see something that is not in compliance with

rules and regulations, do not wait to report it to the school authorities immediately.

These are just some ideas as to how you can improve your child's safety and increase communication between you and your child. Always keep your eyes open to anything that doesn't seem quite right. Here again I am talking about your instinct—trust and follow it always.

Worst Comes to Worst

In spite of everything we talked about, being alert and aware about your safety, self-defense tips, building strength and stamina, there are still no guarantees that you will be able to prevent a crime from happening. So what do you do if the worst comes to worst?

Preserving Evidence

So far we have been focusing on avoiding and preventing rape. If, in spite of all the precautions and measures you have undertaken, you are still assaulted and/or raped, the first thing you need to do is get yourself to safety.

If your cell phone is still with you, call a person you can trust (perhaps your ICE contacts). Getting to safety can be going to your own house or to that of a trusted friend or family member or even straight to the hospital. The choice you make will depend on the circumstances under which the crime took place and the extent of your injuries. You may go directly to the hospital and meet your family or friends there. The other choice is to call the police right away. Having said that, this is not always the easiest or the first thought that comes to the victim's mind.

Once you have reached a safe environment, you need to get medical attention immediately. From this point onwards you need to preserve as much forensic evidence as possible. Even if you just want to get into the shower and scrub yourself clean, I urge you not to as valuable evidence under your nails, on your clothes, hair and private parts will be lost. It is important to preserve DNA evidence, which could be essential in establishing the identity of your attacker or rapist, and also play an important role in convicting him. In fact, many police forces around the country, including the Delhi Police is making DNA profiling of attackers a mandatory part of rape investigations if the identity of the attacker is unknown or if the victim is a minor. Here is the list of things *not* to do in order to preserve evidence.

What Not to Do Before an Examination:

- Bathe or shower
- Change clothes

- Use the restroom (if you really have to go, preserve the contents in a plastic container)
- Comb your hair

Once in the hospital, you need to state that you have been a victim of sexual assault and that you need medical attention. This will ensure that the hospital personnel conduct a proper examination with the aim of collecting as much forensic evidence as possible, including DNA samples in a clean plastic bag or a rape kit.

You may or may not decide to report the crime right away, but getting a medical exam and subsequently keeping the evidence safe from damage will ensure that if you decide to report the crime later, it will enable the police to access and test the evidence.

At this point, a report should be made describing the events as they happened. It is quite possible that you will need to narrate or write down the course of events a few times. Going through the examination right after the rape as well as having to relive it by narrating it and writing down the course of events in presence of strangers is an extremely emotionally traumatic experience. However, I would strongly advise you to go through it, as this can ensure that you get justice for the crime against you and that the perpetrator is punished and taken off the streets. By doing this, not only can you save another person from going through the experience, you can ensure that this doesn't happen to you again. In many ways, this is the first step towards the healing process.

Writing a Report

Try to remember and narrate the sequence of events as they happened (chronologically) with as many details as possible about the incident. Write in simple language and take as much time as you need to complete it.

Begin by stating the date, time, and location/city. Describe the events that led to the incident. For example, 'You were on your way from work when he approached you', etc. Describe the conversation he had with you or if there were more men, what they were talking about. Describe the location where the incident happened (this can lead to more forensic evidence and bring clarity about the jurisdiction). Description of the location should also have as many details as possible.

Describe the attacker in as many details as possible.
- What was his built?
- What was his height?
- What was his weight?
- What colour were his hair and eyes?
- Did he have facial and/or bodily hair?
- Did he have any distinguishing marks on his face or body (moles, scars, growths on the face or body)?

- Did he have any tattoos (sometimes parents in rural India tattoo names of the children on the children's forearms)?
- Had he mentioned anything about himself, his name, or place of his birth?
- Did he speak in a distinctive accent or dialect?
- Did he have any speech impairments?

All of this can help the police build an accurate profile of the attacker which can lead to a quick arrest. The end of the report should contain all the steps you took before getting medical attention.

Please be patient and prepared to clarify some parts of your statement. Keep in mind that the police may appear quite cold and insensitive even when asking relevant and valid questions. Huge efforts have been made in order to minimize the trauma that rape victims go through when being examined and filing reports, as well as to equip the police and medical teams with additional training as to how to handle rape victims. However, in spite of clear guidelines being issued on these rights and regulations we still read about the insensitivities of police and hospital staff. Keep in mind that they are on your side and are helping you create a report with as many relevant details as possible to nab the perpetrator. On the other hand, if the police does not record the information given to them by the victim, which is then approved and signed by the victim, it is a criminal offence punishable with a prison sentence under The Criminal Law (Amendment) Act 2013.

What After

Unfortunately this is not where it ends. For many rape victims, once things seemingly settle down is when the real battle starts. First there could be physical injuries to the body as well as danger of contracting any of number of Sexually Transmitted Diseases (STD), so the first aspect is Physical Healing. The second one deals with an Emotional Trauma and Healing.

Step 1: *Physical Healing*

Apart from being physically injured and having to do regular checkups to monitor wounds and injuries, the rape victim also has to closely monitor for any signs of a pregnancy and symptoms of STDs.

When it comes to pregnancy, this can be dealt with by taking a morning after pill, which is effective up to 72 to 120 hours after the incident. Having said that, as rape is a very different experience which can have many other injuries accompanying the sexual intercourse including the violence of the intercourse, this option should be considered under medical advice and doctor's guidance only.

HIV would probably be the most serious threat, signs of which can be tested fairly accurately only after twelve weeks following the rape. Here is a list of the most common STDs and the time it takes for the symptoms to manifest.

Average Time from Exposure to Symptoms for Some Common STDs:

- **HIV:** It may take up to six months after exposure to the HIV virus before you will test positive on an HIV antibody test, although most infected people will test positive within three months. A negative test, therefore, isn't a reliable indicator of your infection status if you were only exposed for a week. Tests that look directly for HIV RNA, the virus' genetic material, can detect an infection earlier, but are harder to find.
- **Chlamydia:** One to three weeks after exposure to the bacteria. Even asymptomatic patients with chlamydia can have complications, so it is important to be regularly screened by your physician.
- **Gonorrhea:** This is frequently asymptomatic. When symptoms do appear, they may show up as early as two days after exposure, or take as long as one month.
- **Syphilis:** The characteristic of the first stage of syphilis appears, on average, twenty-one days after infection, but may appear any time between ten to ninety days after exposure to the bacterium.
- **Chancroid:** Symptoms of Chancroid may appear any time from one day to several weeks after infection. Most people find that lesions appear within five to seven days.
- **Trichomoniasis:** Although most men never have symptoms of Trichomoniasis, in women symptoms usually appear between five to twenty-eight days after exposure.

- **Scabies:** If you have never had scabies before, it may take one to two months for symptoms to appear. However, if you have previously been infected, symptoms may show after only a couple of days.
- **Genital Warts:** Most people who are going to have symptomatic genital warts will experience their first outbreak within three months of initial infection.
- **Genital Herpes:** Although most people never know they're infected. If they are then symptoms show within two weeks of exposure to the virus. Some people will also experience a fever and full-body viral symptoms around that time.
- **Hepatitis B:** Symptoms of hepatitis B usually show up between four to six weeks after infection. However, hepatitis B is completely preventable by vaccination.
- *Molloscum Contagiosum:* Scientists are uncertain of the incubation period of *Molluscum contagiosum*. Current estimates range from two weeks to six months.

Step 2: Emotional Healing

Rape is an extremely traumatic experience for the survivor and this book would not be complete if we don't address the emotional impact and healing aspects as well. In the 1970s, two ladies, Ann Wolbert Burgess and Lynda Lytle Holmstrom, coined the term Rape Trauma Syndrome (RTS). RTS is described as a group of emotional responses to the trauma of rape that a survivor undergoes. According to experts, there are between two and three phases of RTS. Having said that there can be many variations and 'sub phases' in each of these, depending on the particular set of circumstances during the assault as well as the particulars of the victim.

The main phases are:

1. **The Acute Phase** happens immediately post the attack and can last for a few days to a few months. In this phase, the victim is trying to process what has happened to her. Here's what a person goes through during this phase:
   - *Expressed*: Person may want to talk about it all the time, or there are bouts of agitation or hysteria, crying spells, or anxiety attacks.
   - *Controlled*: Person acting as though 'everything is fine' and 'nothing happened'. There are no visible emotions. This can also be due to shock.
   - *Shock/disbelief*: There is a strong sense of disorientation of the survivor.

In this stage, some of the following behaviours are also manifested:
- confusion and crying
- hysteria
- diminished alertness and numbness
- lack of memory and inability to concentrate
- disorganized thought content

- nausea and vomiting
- anxiety and bodily tremors, feeling of paralyzing fear
- obsession to wash or clean themselves
- sensitivity to other people's reactions

2. **The Outward Adjustment Phase** is when survivors try to get back to their day-to-day lives but still suffer inside. This can last for a few years.

   There are many ways this phase can manifest itself. From mood swings, which can swing from fear to anger, from feeling helpless to humiliated, dirty, unworthy, depressed, etc. the list is complicated and endless. The bottomline is that every emotional response is valid and justified and the survivor is entitled to them. Often, survivors experience physical pain which could be from the physical injuries or could be psycho-somatic—they experience sleep-related problems and loss of appetite or could become prone to bingeing. They could easily show a strong reaction to being touched and having flashbacks of the assault, which can result in a loss of previously close relationships. Many women experience difficulties resuming their normal sexual life.

   In this stage, some of the following behaviours are manifested:
   - *Minimization of the attack*: It could have been worse, and everything is fine.
   - *Dramatization*: The assault starts to dominate the survivor's life and she cannot stop talking about it.

- *Suppression*: Refusal to discuss the incident and behaves as though nothing happened.
- *Explanation*: Trying to analyze all aspects of the assault—who had done what and what the rapist may have been thinking or feeling.
- *Flight*: In order to escape the pain she tries to disconnect with her previous life, either by moving or changing jobs or her personal appearance.

Survivors often stop viewing the world as a safe place and their personal sense of security is disturbed, therefore it is very important to have a good support system during this phase, family, close friends, and support groups can give a much needed sense of security and familiarity. This is also a time when the victim should seek professional help, either from a counselor, psychiatrist, or a social worker with experience to help deal with the trauma.

Recovery

The physical well-being of the survivor is often overlooked in these cases. It is important to eat regularly and to get adequate nutrition. Here are a few things that are crucial to recovery and need to be given importance.
- Exercise is often the most overlooked aspect of self-care. Try to exercise at least for 30 minutes, three times a week. Exercise can help regulate moods—it

can help the survivor tire themselves out enough to get adequate sleep.
- Proper sleep will go a long way for physical and emotional recovery. In the short-term, the survivor may need prescriptive medicines to help in sleeping. However, over a period of time the sleeping pattern will get re-established.
- Meditation and deep breathing can definitely help find a new emotional and mental equilibrium.

3. **The Resolution/Renewal/Renormalization Phase:** This is the final phase where the assault is no longer the central focus of the survivor's life. The victim starts to enjoy life and see positive things around her again. Feelings of self blame and shame are resolved and while the incident is not forgotten, it does not cause as much pain as it once did and the victim is able to accept the assault as a part of her past and life and is able to move on.

APPENDIX

APPENDIX

Appendix 1

Safety Apps

The modern day and age has many advantages, technology probably being the most important one. Safety smart phone apps came as a result of an attempt to create a quicker support and warning system, which can save more lives. Here is a list as of some current prominent apps which are active and working in India. I am sure that in the near future we will have many more and I apologize if I have omitted any. The intention was to set you onto the right path and not to claim this is all there is.

Hollaback

'Hollaback! You have the power to end street harassment', is the tag line of this particular app. Users can take a photo of the harasser and upload it as 'caught in the act' and submit their story on ihollaback.org. It signals the perpetrator that his photo is shared on the website. The app encourages users to submit stories along with photographs of street harassment at every level from catcalls to being groped or even individuals exposing themselves in public. It is a free version which is available in both iPhone and Android phones. Apart from the apps and website, Hollaback is part of an international movement with locally based Hollaback organizations in major cities and metropolitan areas across eighteen countries. It tries to create a crowd-sourced initiative to end street harassment and break the silence which generally surrounds these issues.

bSafe

The bSafe app works as a guardian that sends an emergency message to chosen contacts with a push of a single button. Its slogan is 'Never Walk Alone'. The free version sets up a safety net of 'Guardians' who can respond immediately to text messages and the subscribed version offers two levels of safety—a Risk mode with real time GPS which tracks the position and a Timer mode with an automatic alarm activation. It's a user-friendly app which just needs a single tap to inform the chosen contacts. The app is available in iOS, Android, and BlackBerry devices and includes both free and advanced versions.

Street Safe

This is a premium app which takes care of security and protection. If you think you are in trouble, Street Safe guides you with a Personal Safety Advisor, a feature called 'Walk with Me', which gets the details of the situation and stays on line until they ensure the user gets back home safe. In case the call is cut, the

Safety Advisor connects the user to the local police for further help and guidance. In case of emergency situations, a feature called 'Silent Alarm' enables you to get local help from real-time location using GPS and physical description of the user. The app is available for free across various platforms in Google Play Store, Apple App Store, BlackBerry, and Windows Phone Store.

Sentinel

It is a smartphone application used to serve as a virtual security guard for women. Users can press a button once they feel they are being stalked or harassed. It sends out instant alerts to let friends, family, or the police know about the trouble and save them. The app is available for about INR 50 on Android and other platforms.

Guardly

This is a personal safety application designed for women which connects with all of the other safety network connections. It differs from—other apps as it places phone calls to those listed contacts along with the name, real-time location and the type of emergencies—'Stroke' or 'Walking Home Alone' helps and also to identify different locations. It has a profile page where the user can include personal information like birth date, eyes and hair colour, weight, height, blood type, and so on. The subscribed version enables responders to connect to conference calls. The paid version includes tracking of real-time location. It is available in iPhone, iPod Touch, Android, BlackBerry, and Windows Phone 7 phones.

FightBack

FightBack, developed by the Mahindra group firm, was initially charged as per usage, but recently after the Delhi gang rape case, the company has started giving free access to the app. It uses GPS, GPRS, SMS, emails, and even Facebook to inform friends in need of help. It also shows the user's location on Google Maps and sends SOS emergency text messages to close and dear ones. The app is available in Android and Nokia phones and for phones which support Java apps.

Fightback—Women's Safety

Nokia's OVI store has shockingly few apps for women's safety. One of the apps we managed to find was the FightBack app. FightBack app is a very basic app similar to ones listed above. However, one unique feature we like about the app is the Facebook status update. Apart from providing SMS and email options to alert the other person during distress, this app also updates your Facebook status. So even if your emergency contacts are unreachable, you can be sure at least someone from your extensive friend list knows about your predicament and will do something to help. Pretty useful we say!

Me Against Rape

Me Against Rape is an app recently developed in India to counter the terrifying attacks faced by women. The app lets users list two emergency contact numbers and sends SMS in times of need to the listed numbers. There are also options for calling/audio recording to save as proof. There is also a location logs feature, which saves your location and sends alerts along with your location information. The information can be accessed even at a later date and be presented as proof.

Suspects Registry–FOR WOMEN

Suspects Registry–FOR WOMEN combines multiple features for women's safety. The app lets women list upto three emergency contacts and sends an SMS in times of need. Alternatively, a 60-second sound recording can also be sent. The app also lets users take images and recordings to submit as proof at a later date. The recordings can immediately be uploaded to the community Facebook page bringing the offense to the notice of millions immediately. The app not only acts as an informant for your near and dear ones but the app makers also promise action against the offenders.

SmartShehar Safety

The SmartShehar Safety app lets users add multiple emergency contacts to their lists. In case of an emergency, the app also lets users take a picture or recording. The picture is immediately emailed to everyone in the emergency contact list. At the same time, the user's location can be sent as an SMS. The app is definitely a must-have for all women!

Damini

This app possesses the features of all the mentioned apps. Users can create a list of emergency contacts and send an SMS, location information is sent at periodic intervals, and also let's users record. Once the app is opened, it automatically begins recording and clips are emailed to emergency contacts. Additionally, these clips are also saved on a cloud service and an SMS with the link to these videos is sent out. This ensures that even if the phone is lost or broken during the attack, the information is not destroyed. The app can also be saved on the phone's speed dial.

WithU

WithU is an emergency app for smartphones which works on the same principles as the other apps. You download it, designate numbers of people who will be your distress contacts (ICE contacts) and after that the only thing you need to do is to press the power button twice and it automatically sends out alert messages every two minutes to designated ICE persons. Apart from a distress message, it also tracks your location and shares your story by uploading the contents online.

Appendix 2

Women's Helpline Numebrs and NGOs

181: National women's helpline number (can be reached by both landline and mobile phones in all states of India)

WOMEN's HELPLINE NUMBERS

No.	Name of the Department	Helpline Number
1.	DCW Helpline	23379181 23370597
2.	Women Helpline	1091 (24 hrs. toll free), 23317002, 23317004, 23411091
3.	Delhi Police Post Box No.	5353 (women in distress can send their complaints through this Post Box)
4.	Police Control Room	100
5.	Transport Helpline	9604-400-400

HELPLINES FOR WOMEN IN DELHI

For Women in Distress

Delhi Commission for Women	23379181/ 23370597
Delhi Police Helplines	1091/1291/ 23317004
JAGORI	26692700
National Commission for Women	23237166/ 23234918
National Human Rights Commission	9810298900/ 23385368
Rahi Foundation (support centre for women survivors of child sexual abuse)	26238466/ 26224042/ 26227647

Legal Aid

Human Rights Law Network	243745501/ 243746922
Lawyer's Collective (Womens Rights Initiative: runs a legal aid cell for domestic violence cases)	24373904/ 24372923
Multiple Action Research Group (MARG)	26497483/ 26496925
Pratidhi	22527259

Shelter Homes/ Hostels for Women

Shakti Shalini	24373737-39
Aashray Adhikar Abhiyan	22481609/ 9868122997

YWCA (hostel for working women)	23362779/ 23362975/ 55367705
Prabha Tara (hostel for working women)	26170680

Counseling/Support Services

Snehi	65978181
Sanjeevani	26862222/ 26864488
Swachetan	26123931/ 26135296/ 9810262767

HELPLINES

For Women in Distress

Central Social Welfare Board—Police Helpline	1091/ 1291 (011) 23317004
Shakti Shalini	10920
Shakti Shalini—women's shelter	(011) 24373736/ 24373737
Saarthank	(011) 26853846/ 26524061
All India Women's Conference	10921/ (011) 23389680
JAGORI	(011) 26692700
Joint Women's Programme (also has branches in Bangalore, Kolkata, Chennai)	(011) 24619821
Sakshi: violence intervention center	(0124) 2562336/ 5018873
Saheli: a women's organization	(011) 24616485 (Saturdays)
Nirmal Niketan	(011) 27859158

Nari Raksha Samiti	(011) 23973949
RAHI Recovering and Healing from Incest. A support centre for women survivors of child sexual abuse	(011) 26238466/ 26224042 26227647

Legal Aid

Human Rights Law Network—runs Madhyam Helpline and provides Legal Services	(011) 24316922/ 24324503
Lawyers Collective Womens Rights Initiative (LC WRI)—runs a pro-bono legal aid cell for domestic violence cases	(011) 24373993/ 24372923
Multiple Action Research Group (MARG)	(011) 26497483/ 26496925
Delhi Police helpline	1091
Delhi Commission for Women	(011) 23379181/ 23370597
Women's Cell, Delhi Police	(011) 24673366/ 4156/ 7699
National Commission for Women	(011) 23237166/ 23236203/ 23236204
National Human Rights Commission	(011) 23385368/9810298900
Pratidhi	(011) 22527259

Helpline for Students

24×7 Anti-ragging Helpline	1800-180-5522/ 155222 helpline@antiragging.net

Helpline for Consumers

National Consumer Helpline	1800-11-4000 (Toll Free)

For Sexuality and Related Issues

TARSHI: Talking about Reproductive and Sexual Health Issues Helpline and Counseling Services	(011) 24372229
Parivar Seva Sanstha	(011) 24335055

For Emotional and Relationship Problems

Sumaitri	(011) 23710763
Sanjeevani (Qutab Institutional Area)	(011) 26862222/ 26864488
Sanjeevani (Defence Colony)	(011) 24318883/ 24311918
SNEHI	(011) 65418181 (O) HELPLINE – (011) 65978181
Swaasthya	(011) 26274690
Depression Helpline	(011) 55258383
IFSHA (Interventions For Support Healing & Awareness)	(011) 26253289

For Children

Ankur	(011) 26523395
Delhi Childline	1098 (Toll Free)
Prayas—for children ages 6-17 years	(011) 29955505/ 26089544/ 29956244/ 29051103

HIV/AIDS

AIDS Awareness Group (AAG)	(011) 26187953/ 26187954
Shubhchintak Helpline (AIIMS)	(011) 26588333

For Lesbian and Bisexual Women

Sangini	(011) 55676450

For Men who Have Sex with Men

Naz Foundation India Trust—provide female and male sexual health services	(011) 26910499/ 51325042

Disability Issues

ASTHA	(011) 26449029/ 30985439

Emergency Trauma Care Helpline

Centralized Accident Trauma Services (CATS)	(011) 23981099/ 23971099/ 1099/ 102

For Senior Citizens

Agewell Foundation	(011) 29836486/ 29840484

Related to Substance Abuse

Narcotics Anonymous (NA)	9818072887
Alcohol Anonymous (AA)	9811908707/ 55604980

ForOther Women's Organizations

Aashray Adhikar Abhiyan	(011) 55281301/ 9868122997
Chetna	9810597427/ (011) 23371962
Chetanalaya (domestic workers' forum)	(011) 26497483/ 26496925
Prayatan	(011) 26524065
Swati—(working women's hostel)	(011) 2336 5974

IN OTHER STATES

WEST BENGAL

SWAYAM 9/2B Deodar Street, Kolkata 700019	(033) 24863367, 24863368

ANDHRA PRADESH

ASMITA 10-3-96, Plot 283, 4th Floor, Street 6, Teacher's Colony, East Maredapally, Secundarabad	(040) 27733745
ANVESHI 2-2-18/49, Durgabai Deshmukh Colony, Baghamberpet, Hyderabad	(040) 2868489

RAJASTHAN

VIVIDHA 335 Mahavir Nagar- II, Maharani Farm, Durgapura, Jaipur	(0141) 2762932

MAHARASHTRA

MAJLIS-MASHWARA A–2 Golden Valley Building, No.4, Opp Canara Bank, Kalina Kurla Road, Kalina, Mumbai	(022) 26180394
AWAAZ-E-NISWAN 84 Samuel Street, (Palagali), Jain High School, 1st Floor, Dongri, Mumbai	(022) 23439421
Women and Law Unit (Legal Aid and Counseling)	(022) 26439029

JHARKHAND

PRERNA BHARTI College Rd., Patherchapti, Post Madhupur, Dist Deoghar	(06438) 24359

GUJARAT

OLAKH 24 Jalaram Park, Opp Lalbahadur Vidyalaya, Harni Road, Baroda	(0265) 2486487
SAHRWARU O–45,46 4th Floor, New York Trade Centre, Near Thaltej Cross Road, Sarkhej-Gandhinagar Highway, Ahmedabad	(079) 6857848, 6858195, 6843395

ASSAM

NORTH EAST NETWORK J.N. Barooah Lane, Guwahati	(0361) 2631582

HIMACHAL PRADESH

JAGORI RURAL RESOURCE CENTRE Near Education Board Colony, Kangra	(01892) 246857

KARNATAKA

VIMOCHANA / ANGALA C/o AWHRC, 33/1-9,10 Thyagaraj Layout, Jai Bharath Nagar, Bangalore	(080) 5492782

KERALA

VIMOCHANA/ANGALA TC 27/2323 Convent Rd, Trivandrum	(0471) 2462251

CHHATTISGARH

CHHATTISGARH MAHILA JAGRITI SANGATHAN 7 Geetanjali Nagar, PO Shanker Nagar, Dist Raipur	(0771) 2420338

UTTAR PRADESH

SAHYOG C 2015 Indira Nagar, Lucknow	(0522) 2387010
VANANGANA Dwarikapuri Colony, Opp Bus Stand, Chitrakoot, Karvi	(05198) 236985
AALI C 33A Sector A, Mahanagar, Lucknow	(0522) 2782066/60

TAMIL NADU

SNEHDI 4 Rangan Street, T Nagar, Chennai	(044) 2446293
THE BANYAN 6th Main Rd., Mogappair Eri Scheme, Chennai	(044) 26530504 / 26530105

MANIPUR

Punshi Lamba (Drop-in Centre) Imphal	(0385) 2422734

CHANDIGARH

SAMVAD	(0172) 2546389

NGOS INVOLVED IN COMBATING VIOLENCE AGAINST WOMEN

No	Name and Address	Telephone/Fax
1.	ALL INDIA WOMEN'S CONFERENCE 6, Bhagwan Das Road, Delhi www.aiwc.org.in	Tel: 23381165 Fax: 23384092
2.	JWP JOINT WOMEN'S PROGRAMME CISRS House, 14, Jangpura–B, Mathura Road, Delhi 110 014	Tel: 24314821 Fax: 24313660
3.	STREEBAL B-5/19, Safdarjung Enclave, Delhi 24 www.streebal.com	Tel: 26164113 Fax: 26160279
4.	YWCA 10, Parliament Street, Delhi 1 www.ywcaindia.org	Tel: 23340294 Fax: 23342220

No	Name and Address	Telephone/Fax
5.	SHAKTI SHALINI 6/30 B, Jangpura-B, Delhi 14	Tel: 24312483 Fax: 24322220
6.	SAKSHI B-64, First Floor, South Extension-II, Delhi 49 www.sakshingo.org	Tel: 24643946, 24623295 Fax: 24643946
7.	JAGORI C-54, Top Floor, South Extension-II, Delhi 49 www.jagori.org	Tel: 26257015 Fax: 26253629/ 7755
8.	NARI RAKSHA SAMITI Raj Niwas Marg, Civil Lines, Delhi 54	Tel: 23973949 Fax: 23973949
9.	NIRANTAR B-64, 2nd Floor, Sarvodaya Enclave, Delhi 17 www.nirantar.net	Tel: 26966334, 26517726
10.	PRATIDHI Police Station Complex, Shakarpur Pushta Marg, Ramesh Park, Delhi 92 www.pratidhi.org	Tel: 22527259, 22450100 Ext.6784
11.	MARG 205-206, 2nd Floor, Shahpur Jat, Delhi 49 www.ngo-marg.org	Tel: 26497483, 26496925
12.	LAWYERS' COLLECTIVE 63/2, FF Masjid RD Jangpura Extension, Delhi 14 www.lawyerscollective.org	Tel: 24316925, 24313904

No	Name and Address	Telephone/Fax
13.	DELHI BROTHERHOOD SOCIETY Brotherhood House 7, Court Lane, Delhi 54	Tel: 23931432 Fax: 23981025
14.	MAHILA DAKSHATA SAMITI 19, Fire Brigade Lane, Opp Campa Cola Factory, Connaught Place, New Delhi www.mahiladakshatasamiti.org	Tel: 23412067
15.	HUMAN RIGHTS LAW NETWORK 65, 2nd Floor, Jangpura, Delhi www.hrln.org	Tel: 24316922, 24324503
16.	NAVJYOTI Vikas Bhawan Sanjay Amar Colony Yamuna Pushta, Delhi 6 www.navjyoti.org.in	Tel: 23866316, 23866403, Fax: 23866312
17.	PRAYATAN E-103, Kalkaji, New Delhi 19	Tel: 26415831, 26022849
18.	ANGAJA FOUNDATION A-7, Amrit Nagar, Behind South Extension-I, Delhi 49 www.angaja.org	Tel: 24645021, 24645022
19.	CENTRE FOR SOCIAL RESEARCH (CSR) 2, Institutional Area, Nelson Mandela Marg C-1, Vasant Kunj, New Delhi 70 www.csrindia.org	Tel: 26899998, 26125583, Fax: 2613782
20.	MAHILA MANDAL INDL COOPERATIVE SOCIETY LTD 961, Mangolpuri, Delhi 110083	Tel: +(91)-(11)- 27918021

No	Name and Address	Telephone/Fax
21.	SANJEEVANI VOLUNTARY ORGANISATION A-6, Satsang Vihar MG, Qutab Institutional Area, Delhi 110016	Tel: +(91)-(11)-26864488
22.	DELHI COMMISSION FOR WOMEN 2nd Flr, Vikas Bhwn, C-Blk, Darya Ganj, Delhi 110002	Tel: +(91)-(11)-23378122
23.	SANJEEVANI SOCIETY FOR MENTAL HEALTH Shopping Centre, Jungpura Side, Defence Colony, Delhi 110024	Tel: +(91)-(11)-24311918
24.	KHAZANI WOMENS POLYTECHNIC 34/18, NR PNB, Devli Rd. Khanpur, Delhi 110062 www.khazaniwomenpolytechnic.com	Tel: +(91)-(11)-41653687
25.	JAGORI WOMEN RESOURCE CENTRE B-114, Shivalik, Malviya Nagar, Delhi 110017	Tel: +(91)-(11)-26691219
26.	SAHARA NGO E-453, Part-II, Greater Kailash, Delhi 110048	Tel: +(91)-(11)-26219147
27.	DELHI MAHILA KALYAN SAMITI 48, Nr D Blk, Institutional Area, Janak Puri, Delhi 110058	Tel: +(91)-(11)-28522851
28.	SEWA BHARAT 7/5, 1st Floor, South Patel Nagar, Delhi 110008	Tel: +(91)-(11)-25840937

No	Name and Address	Telephone/Fax
29.	TARSHI HELPLINE A-91, 1st Floor, Amrit Puti, East of Kailash, Delhi 110065 www.tarshi.net	Tel: +(91)-(11)-26472229
30.	CATHOLIC RELIEF SERVICES 139, Shopping Complex, Zamrudpur, Delhi 110048 www.crs.org	Tel: +(91)-(11)-47674220
31.	INDIAN SOCIAL SECURITY 113, Mohan Singh Place, Connaught Place, Delhi 110001 www.indiansocialsecurity.org	Tel: +(91)-(11)-43077786
32.	SHAKTI VAHINI H-11, 2nd Floor, Hudson Lane, Kingsway Camp, Delhi www.shaktivahini.org	Tel: 9582909025, 42870188
33.	MAITRI J-92, Anant Ram Dairy Complex, R K Puram, Sector - 13, Delhi 110066 www.maitri.india@maitri.org.in	Tel: +91-11-2412-2692 Fax: +91-11-2410-9616

ORGANIZATIONS THAT OFFER COUNSELLING SERVICES FOR WOMEN FACING VIOLENCE

MUMBAI

Women's Centre
104 B, Sunrise Apartment, Nehru Road, Vakola, Santacruz (East), Mumbai 400 055
Ph: 26685997
womcentr@vsnl.com

Maitra Helpline
Shri Ganesh Darshan, 9th Floor, IPH, L.B.S. Marg,
Opp Maharashtra Flywood Centre, Hari Niwas Circle,
Naupada, Thane (W)
Ph: 25433270, 25366577

Special Cell for Women and Children
Office of the Commissioner of Police, Police Head Quarter,
Room no: 36, A block, Gate no 5, Opp.Crawford Market, Mumbai 400 001
Ph: 22620111 Extn: 206
rc_vaw@tiss.edu

Special Cell for Women and Children
Dadar Police Station, Bhawani Shankar Road,
Shaitan Chowky, Dadar (W), Mumbai 400 028
Ph: 2494 0303 Extn: 181, 24691681

Special Cell for Women and Children
Kandivali Police Station, Swami Vivekananda Road,
Opp Shatabdi Hospital, Kandivali (W), Mumbai 400 067
Ph: 24691753

Special Cell for Women and Children
C.B.D. Belapur Police Station, Sector – 1, Opp C.B.D. Belapur Bus Depot, Navi Mumbai 400 614
Ph: 2758 0255

SNEHA (Society for Nutrition Education & Health Action)
Urban Health Centre Dharavi, Mumbai 17
Ph: 24042627, 24040045

Sakhya Women Guidance Cell
The Image - 1st Floor, Nirmal Naka, Nalasopara,
Taluka - Vasai, Dist Thane
Ph: 95250 2471540
mcfhi@vsnl.net

Sakhya Women Guidance Cell
Thane Civil Hospital, Ground Floor
Contact person: Ms Jyoti
Ph: 9224642560

Awaz E Niswan
151, Princess building, Flat - 13, 1st Floor,
R. Bhatt Marg, Opp J J hosp, Mumbai 3
Ph: 2375840, 23758462
niswan@vsnl.net

Awaz E Niswan
Rehnuma Library Centre
Darulfala Building, 1st floor, C Wing, Room no. 102,
Mumbra, Kausa
Ph: 25490038

Stree Mukti Sanghatana
Shramik, Royal Crest, Lokmanya Tilak Vasahat
Road no. 3. Dadar (East)
Ph: 24174381

Stree Mukti Sanghatana
Family Counselling Centre, Near Matoshri Ramabai Ambedkar
Marternity Home,
Ramkrishna Chemburkar Road, Chembur Naka,

Mumbai 400 071
Ph: 25297198

Stree Mukti Sanghatana
Family Counselling Centre, Sector 3,
Cidco Communication Centre, Near Vashi Police Station, Vashi
Ph: 27821564

Swadhar
Keshav Gore Smaarak Trust, Arye Road, Goregaon (W)
Mumbai 400 062
Ph: 28720638

Aasra
A 4, Tanwar View, CHS, Plot 43, Sector 7, Koparkhairane,
New Mumbai 400701
Ph: 27546669

Dilaasa
Dept. no. 101, Opp. Casualty, K.B. Bhabha Hospital,
Bandra (W), Mumbai 400 050.
Ph: 26400229 (Direct)
26422775 / 26422541 Extn. 4376 / 4511
dilaasa@vsnl.net

Dilaasa
Dept. no. 15, K.B. Bhabha Municipal Hospital, Belgrami Road,
Kurla (W), Mumbai 400070
Ph: 26500241 Extn. 212

PUNE

Susamvad—Sakhi - Helpline
B1 Seema Apt, Shirole Path, Opp Fergusson College Main Gate,
Pune 4
Ph: 9520 25448400, 25538434

Asha Sanstha
Action for Self Reliance Hope and Awareness
Vishrmbag Police Station, Farasakhana Building, 3rd Floor,
Bhudhwar Chowk, Pune 411002
Ph: 9520 24484535
ngoasha@gmail.com

Nari Samata Manch
473, Sadashiv Peth, Pune 411030
Ph: 9520 24473116
nsm@pn3.vsnl.net.in

Masum
Masum Sanchalit Sanvad, Family Counselling and
Guidance Centre, Malsa Kant Society, Saswad,
Taluka - Purandhar, Pune
Ph: 02115 222969

Swadhar
C/o Niwara Devid sasun Anath Pangu Graha,
96, Navi Peth, Pune 30
Ph: 9520 24533452
swadhar@rediffmail.com

Chetna Mahila Mandal
13, Gururaj Society, Bhosari, Pune 411039
Ph: 9520 26610516
jyotipathania@yahoo.co.in

Maher
Bhima Koregaon, Vadu Budruk,
Taluka Shirud, Pune 412216
Ph: 952137 252174
maheropn3@vsnl.net.in

Shramik Mahila Morcha
101, Shivajinagar, Pune 5
Ph: 9520 25533560, 25534652
M: 09422530186
R: 24452053

DELHI

Jagori—A Women's Organization
C-54 South Extension II, New Delhi
Ph: 91 11 2669 1219, 91 11 2669 1220
jagori@jagori.org

Action India
5/27A, Jangpura - B, Behind Rajdoot Hotel,
New Delhi 110014
Ph: 91 11 24377470, 24374785
actionindia@vsnl.com actioni@hotmail.com

Tarshi
11 - Mathura Road, 1st Floor, Jangpura B, New Delhi 110014
Ph: 91 11 24379070, 24379071
tarshi@vsnl.com

Shakti Shalini
6/30-B, Lower Ground Floor,
Kargil Park Lane, Jangpura-B, New Delhi 110014
Ph: 91 11 24373636, 24373736
shakishalini@mantraonline.com

Rahi Foundation
RAHI Foundation, M 50 Chitaranjan Park
Ground Floor, New Delhi 110019
Ph: 011 40536176
rahifoundation@gmail.com

BANGALORE

Vimochana
33/1-10 Thyagraj Layout, Jaibharath Nagar,
Bangalore 560033
Ph: 080 25492783
streelekha@vsnl.net

Hengasara Hakkina Sangha
No. 1024, 38th Cross, 25th Main, 4th T block,
Jaya Nagar Bangalore 41
Ph: 080 26639884
hhs@bgl.vsnl.net.in

KOLKATTA

Swayam
9/2 B Deodar Street
Kolkata 700019, West Bengal
Ph: 91 33 2486 3367/3368/3357
swayam@cal.vsnl.net.in

GUJARAT/KUTCH

Kutch Mahila Vikas Sanghatna
11, Nutan Colony, Bhuj, Kutch 370001
Ph: 02832 222124, 223311
kmvsbhuj@gmail.com, preetinbsoni@gmail.com

Abdasa Mahila Vikas Sanghatana
Shiddheshwar Nagar, Bhind Post Office,
Naliya Kutch 370001
Ph: 028314 222165

Ujas Mahila Vikas Sanghatana—Mundra District
Sadou Road, KVK Campus, Mundra, Kutch
Ph: 02838 223104

Centre for Social Justice, Bhuj
10, Meghmaya, Shardha Society, Bhuj, Kutch
Ph: 02832 223441
csjkutch@rediffmail.com

VADODARA

Olakh—A space for women
A Feminist Documentation Resource and Counseling Centre
8-A, Nivruti Colony, Opp Jila Talim Bhavan, Karelibaug, Vadodara
Ph: 0265 2486487, 2466037

JAIPUR

Vishakha
9 Pratap Nagar, Near Glass Factory, Tonk Road, Jaipur
Ph: 0141 517 2422

Vividha
Mahila Salaha Evam Surakshan Kendra (South),
Gandhi Nagar, Mahila Thana, Gandhi Nagar, Jaipur
Ph: 0141 5172435
vividha_2001@yahoo.com

Vividha
Mahila Salaha Evam Surakshan Kendra (North),
Mahila Thana (North, Dhabai Ji Ki Haveli, Hawa Mahal Road,
Jaipur
Ph: 0141 5172008

MADHYA PRADESH, BHOPAL

Sangini—Gender Resource Center
G 3/385, Gulmohar Colony,
Bhopal 462039
Ph: 0755 4276158
sanginicenter@rediffmail.com

MEGHALAYA

Voluntary Health Association
Opposite Iarisa Cottage, Upper Nongrim Hills,
Shillong 793003
Ph: 0364 2522834, 2522835 (Office)
bj1975@rediffmail.com, vhamegh@rediffmail.com

Lympung Ki Seng Kynthei
Ph: 0364 2504233, 2220595

UTTAR PRADESH, LUCKNOW

Sahayog
A-240 Indira Nagar, Lucknow 226016
Ph: 91522 2341319, 2310747

Humsafar
Support Centre For Women
27, New Berry Road (near Times of India)
Lucknow 226001

Appendix 3

Police Helpline Numbers

DELHI
Police Control Room Number　　　　　100
Women's Helpline　　　　　　　　　　1091

CAW CELL TELEPHONE NUMBERS

No.	Name of the Office	Telephone No.
1.	Jt. CP/CAW CELL ,NANAKPURA	26882691
2.	DCP/CAW CEL, NANAKPURA	26883769
3.	ACP OF CAW/CELL, NANAKPURA	26883650 26880393 24121777 24674156 24677699 24100010
4.	DUTY OFFICER NANAKPURA	24673366

No.	Name of the Office	Telephone No.
5.	ACP/EAST DISTRICT	22091950
6.	ACP/NORTH EAST DISTRICT	22137210
7.	ACP/CENTRE DISTRICT	22365753
8.	ACP/NORTH DISTRICT	23697610
9.	ACP/NORTH WEST DISTRICT	27323566
10.	ACP/SOUTH DISTRICT	26482871
11.	ACP/SOUTH WEST DISTRICT	25088987
12.	ACP/WEST DISTRICT	25915314
13.	ACP/NEW DELHI DISTRICT	22322426

WOMEN'S HELPLINE NUMBERS: DELHI POLICE STATION WISE

CENTRAL RANGE

Central District

No.	Name of Police Station and Women Helpline No.
1.	PS Darya Ganj 23240100
2.	PS Jama Masjid 23247100
3.	PS Chandni Mahal 23243100
4.	PS Kamla Market 23234524
5.	PS Hauq Qazi 23234523
6.	PS I P Estate 23370999
7.	PS Pahar Ganj 23636100
8.	PS Nabi Karim 23521300
9.	PS DBG Road 23635100
10.	PS Karol Bagh 28721115
11.	PS Rajinder Nagar 28745100
12.	PS Prasad Nagar 25711110

No.	Name of Police Station and Women Helpline No.
13.	PS Patel Nagar 25871110
14.	PS Anand Parbat 28764279
15.	PS Ranjit Nagar 25702400

New Delhi District

No.	Name of Police Station and Women Helpline No.
1.	Chanakya Puri 23015195
2.	Tuglak Road 23015501
3.	Tilak Marg 23387002
4.	Barakhamba Road 23363899
5.	Connaught Place 23363898
6.	Mandir Marg 23343800
7.	Parliament Street 23361102

North District

No.	Name of Police Station and Women Helpline No.
1.	Subzi Mandi 23827100
2.	Lahori Gate 23957100
3.	Civil Lines 23817100
4.	Bara Hindu Rao 23525100
5.	Sarai Rohilla 23695100
6.	Kashmiri Gate 23917100
7.	Sadar Bazar 23625100
8.	Gulabi Bagh 23645100
9.	Timar Pur 23818100
10.	Kotwali 23987100
11.	Roop Nagar 23844633
12.	Maurice Nagar 27662234
13.	Burari 27616234

NORTHERN RANGE

North-West District

No.	Name of Police Station and Women Helpline No.
1.	PS Ashok Vihar 27220021
2.	PS Keshav Puram 27151723
3.	PS Bharat Nagar 27303222
4.	PS Subhash Place 27351724
5.	PS Rani Bagh 27010525
6.	PS Maurya Enclave 27314426
7.	PS Shalimar Bagh 27495527
8.	PS Mahendra Park 27631128
9.	PS Jahangir Puri 27631129
10.	PS Bhalswa Dairy 27811230
11.	PS Swaroop Nagar 27811231
12.	PS Model Town 27120032
13.	PS Adarsh Nagar 27672933
14.	PS Mukherjee Nagar 27653334

Outer District

No.	Name of Police Station and Women Helpline No.
1.	PS Narela 27281521
2.	PS Alipur 27202322
3.	PS Samaipur Badli 27852123
4.	PS Prashant Vihar 27555524
5.	PS South Rohini 27943025
6.	PS Mangol Puri 27913026
7.	PS Vijay Vihar 27041227

No.	Name of Police Station and Women Helpline No.
8.	PS Sultan Puri 25961628
9.	PS Aman Vihar 25961629
10.	PS Bawana 27751331
11.	PS Shahbad Dairy 27822132
12.	PS K N Katju Marg 27570233
13.	PS North Rohini 27041334
14.	PS Begumpur 27581112
15.	PS Kanjhawala 25951925

SOUTH WESTERN RANGE

South District

No.	Name of Police Station and Women Helpline No.
1.	Hauz Khas 26566564
2.	Saket 29564560
3.	Malviya Nagar 26692505
4.	Defence Colony 26250100
5.	Lodhi Colony 24625200
6.	K M Pur 24624000
7.	Vasant Vihar 26155198
8.	Vasant Kunj North 26123835
9.	Vasant Kunj South 26123854
10.	S J Enclave 24673281
11.	R K Puram 26100181
12.	Sarojini Nagar 24673283
13.	South Campus 26170181
14.	Mehrauli 26646446
15.	Fateh Pur Beri 26659711
16.	Neb Sarai 29554866

South West District

No.	Name of Police Station and Women Helpline No.
1.	Dwarka (South) 28086398
2.	Dwarka (North) 28086401
3.	Dwarka (Sec 23) 28053570
4.	Kapashera 25060098
5.	Najafgarh 25016300
6.	Jaffar Pur Kalan 25318500
7.	Chhawla 25319100
8.	B H D Nagar 28019100
9.	Dabri 25630178
10.	Binda Pur 25630177
11.	Palam Village 25362560
12.	Sagar Pur 25035357
13.	Delhi Cantt 25683837
14.	Naraina 25892800
15.	Inder Puri 25832400

West District

No.	Name of Police Station and Women Helpline No.
1.	PS Rajouri Garden 25937200
2.	PS Kirti Nagar 25937273
3.	PS Moti Nagar 25937400
4.	PS Khyala 25937374
5.	PS Punjabi Bagh 25225200
6.	PS Paschim Vihar 25279200
7.	PS Mianwali Nagar 25278900

No.	Name of Police Station and Women Helpline No.
8.	PS Tilak Nagar 25408222
9.	PS Hari Nagar 28523677
10.	PS Maya Puri 28113833
11.	PS Vikas Puri 25616171
12.	PS Janak Puri 25542199
13.	PS Uttam Nagar 25357324
14.	PS Nangloi 25944700
15.	PS Nihal Vihar 25946720
16.	PS Ranhola 28363004
17.	PS Mundka 28342009

SOUTH EASTERN RANGE

East District

No.	Name of Police Station and Women Helpline No.
1.	PS Farsh Bazar 22381181
2.	PS Vivek Vihar 22140181
3.	PS Anand Vihar 22391181
4.	PS Gazipur 22620181
5.	PS Kalyan Puri 22782181
6.	PS Mayur Vihar 22710988
7.	PS Mandawali 22781181
8.	PS Madhu Vihar 22783181
9.	PS Pandav Nagar 22785181
10.	PS Jagat Puri 22503100
11.	PS Preet Vihar 22506100

No.	Name of Police Station and Women Helpline No.
12.	PS Shakar Pur 22504100
13.	PS Krishna Nagar 22090181
14.	PS Gandhi Nagar 22070181
15.	PS Geeta Colony 22502100
16.	PS New Ashok Nagar

North East District

No.	Name of Police Station and Women Helpline No.
1.	Seelam Pur 22195181
2.	New Usman Pur 22865181
3.	Bhajan Pura 22185181
4.	Gokal Puri 22175181
5.	Khajuri Khas 22962181
6.	G T B Enclave 22570181
7.	Shahdara 22321181
8.	Harsh Vihar 22345181
9.	Nand Nagri 22135722
10.	Seema Puri 22120181
11.	Welcome 22832181
12.	Karawal Nagar 22932181
13.	Jafrabad 22855181
14.	Jyoti Nagar 22800181
15.	M S Park 22121181
16.	Sonia Vihar 24533239

South East District

No.	Name of Police Station and Women Helpline No.
1.	PS Jait Pur 29944300
2.	PS Badar Pur 26998100
3.	PS Ambedkar Nagar 29053100
4.	PS C R Park 26276100
5.	PS Sangam Vihar 26045100
6.	PS Govind Puri 29989100
7.	PS Kalkaji 26430100
8.	PS Lajpat Nagar 29843100
9.	PS Amar Colony 26440100
10.	PS Greater Kailash 29240100
11.	PS New Friends Colony 26926100
12.	PS H N Din 24352000
13.	PS Jamia Nagar 26986100
14.	PS Sunlight Colony 26344100
15.	PS Sarita Vihar 26826100
16.	PS Pul Prahlad Pur 26366100
17.	PS Okhla Ind. Area 26810100

WOMEN'S HELPLINES

Delhi Commission for Women Rape Crisis Helpline	+91-11-23370557

For Women in Distress

Central Social Welfare Board Police Helpline	1091/ 1291/ 011 23317004
Shakti Shalini	10920
Shakti Shalini Women's Shelter	011 24373736/ 24373737
SAARTHAK	011 26853846/ 26524061
All India's Women's Conference	10921/ 011 23389680
JAGORI	011 26692700
Joint Women's Programme (also branches in Bangalore, Kolkata, and Chennai)	011 24619821
Sakshi—Violence Intervention Center	0124 2562336 / 5018873
Saheli—A Women's Organization	011 24616485 (Saturdays)
Nirmal Niketan	011 27859158
Nari Raksha Samiti	011 23973949

Mental Health and Trauma

Snehi	011 26521415, 011 26521494
Sanjeevani	011 26862222/4488 (Qutub Instl Area) 011 24318883, 24311918 (Jangpura)
Swanchetan	011 26123931, 26135296. 9810262767

- **Jagori**: Women's Training, Documentation, Communication and Resource Centre
  B-114, Shivalik, Malviya Nagar
  Ph: 26691219, 2669 1220
  Victim services: a counseling center and support group for women survivors of violence.
  Helpline: 011 2669 2700 (Mon to Fri, 9.30 to 5.30)
  helpline@jagori.org

- **Sakshi:** A Violence Intervention for Women and Children. Works on sexual harassment, sexual assault, child sexual abuse and domestic violence.
  B-67 South Extension Part-1, First Floor
  Ph: 4643946, 4623295
  s.sakshi@mailcity.com

- **Women's Rights Initiative**: runs a pro-bono legal aid cell for domestic violence cases and are also associated with law reforms in the area of domestic violence.
  1st Floor, Masjid Road, Jungpura
  Ph: 4316925, 4313904, 432101
  wri@vsnl.net

MUMBAI

Helpline Numbers for Women in Distress

- 103: The latest women helpline number to complain about eve teasing and any to learn about women self defense.

- Mumbai Police Helplines for Molestation: 103/1090/ 7738133133, 7738144144

- 1298: This number will connect women in distress to relevant NGO's.

- Family Service Center: 22828862

- Women's Center: 26140403

- Latest number for sexual harassment in bus: 1800227550 (Initiative by BEST bus services in Mumbai for women safety)

- **SNEHA Mumbai:** They help and addresses special needs of slum Woman and children and works towards improving their health.
  Ph: 24042627, 24086011
  Crisis helpline: 24040045
  snehamumbai@snehamumbai.org

- **MAJLIS Mumbai:** is a legal and cultural resource centre working in the area of women and minority rights
  Ph: 26662394, 26661252
  Police Helpline for Women
  103: This is a special police helpline who takes action on crime against women through police intervention.
- **Women Right Initiative:** This organization runs a pro bono (free) legal aid cell for domestic violence cases.
  Ph: 43411603/ 43411604
  wri.bombay@lawyerscollective.org
  www.lawyerscollective.org/wri

- **Human Rights Law Network:** works on issues such as woman's justice like
  HIV/AIDS, etc.

Ph: 23439754, 23436692
huright@vsnl.com
www.hrln.org/hrln/

- **SNEHA**: works to empower women/children in poor urban communities. SNEHA's Center for Vulnerable Women and Children specifically provides services (including counseling, legal assistance and community organizing) to women and children experiencing domestic violence.
  310, 3rd Floor, Urban Health Center,
  60 Feet Road, Dharavi, Mumbai 400 017
  Crisis Helpline: 022 2404 0045
  Ph: 022 2404 2627, 2408 6011

- **Swaadhar**, Bombay (Jyoi Kelkar) 872 0638

CHENNAI

- **International Foundation for Crime Prevention and Victim Care (PCVC)**
  Crisis-line: 044 43111143
  pcvc2000@yahoo.com

- **SNEHA**: voluntary organization offering emotional support to the lonely, depressed and suicidal. SNEHA is open 365 days a year and services are free.
  Park View Road, R.A. Puram
  Visit: 8 am to 10 pm at 11
  Ph: 044 24650050 (24 hours a day)

BANGALORE

- **Bangalore Police Helpline:** 1091/ 10928
- **Vimochana**: Helps women with issues ranging from domestic violence sexual harassment at work. Provides counseling, service provision, education/outreach, mobilizing/organizing, activism.
  2124 16th B Main 1-A Cross, HAL IInd Stage
  Ph: (city code = 80) 526 9307
- **Anweshi Women's Counselling Centre**: Runs a counseling, mediation and resource center for women in an abusive situation. If you are writing to them, please enclose a self-addressed envelope with sufficient postage.
  Near YWCA, Cannanore Road, Kozhikode 673 001

KOLKATA

- Sachetna, 31, Mahairban Road
- Socio-Legal Aid Research and Training Center: P-112 Lake Terrace
- Pragatisheel Mahila Manch: 11 N. Ho Chi Minh Road, Sarania, Behala
- Swayam: 9/2 B Deodar Street
  Ph: 2486 3367, 2486 3378, 2486 3357
  swayam@cal.vsnl.net.in

EMERGENCY HELPLINE FOR WOMEN
1091
ONLY FROM A BSNL LANDLINE

Quick safe exit

AVAILABLE 24 HOURS TO HELP

Aashraya (Andhra Mahila Sabha)	Short-stay shelter home, counselling, legal aid, medical and psychiatric support	044-24642566 (24 hours)	12, Rosary Church Road Santhome Chennai 600 004 (drop-in 24 hours)
Annai Fathima Child Welfare Centre	Phone counselling	9444444874 (24 hours)	No. 34, East Mada Street Mylapore Chennai 600 004
Aruwe	Counselling and referral services, legal aid, psychiatric support	044-26454615 (24 hours)	11, Solaiamman Koil St. Ayanavaram, Chennai 600 023
PCVC (International Foundation for Crime Prevention and Victim Care) pcvc2000@yahoo.com	Shanthi Crisis Line, shelters or other emergency residential facilities, medical services, transportation networks, assistance in finding housing or relocating, other emotional support, legal assistance	044-43111143 (24 hours)	2030, First Floor, 13th Main Road Anna Nagar West Chennai 600040.

Sneha help@snehaindia.org	Emotional support to the depressed, desperate and suicidal	044-24640050 (24 hours)	11, Park View Road R.A. Puram, Chennai 600028. (drop-in 8am to 10pm)
ALSO AVAILABLE TO HELP WOMEN IN DISTRESS			
Kalaiselvi Karunalaya Social Welfare Society info@kkssindia.org	Short-stay shelter home, legal clinic, counselling	044-26257779/ 044-26254956	3/PP1, Mogappair West Chennai 600 037 (Near MGR Statue)
Rishi Abhaya Nilayam	Short stay home for young women and girls	044-24981679	36/187, Kutchery Road Mylapore Chennai 600 004.
Sahodari (YWCA) sahodari@ywcamadras.org	Short-stay shelter home, counselling, legal aid, medical and psychiatric support	044-25321737	1086 Poonamallee High Rd Chennai 600084 Shelter services open 6am to 11pm

Appendix 4

Laws and Acts Under the Indian Penal Code (IPC)

Rape Law and Definition Under IPC

Rape is a most heinous crime against women usually involving sexual intercourse which is initiated by one or more persons against another person without that persons consent. The act may be carried out by physical force, coercion, abuse of authority or with a person who is incapable of valid consent, such as one who is unconscious, incapacitated, or below the legal age of consent.

Indian law treats rape as a criminal offence. It falls under criminal law in India. The Indian Penal Code (IPC Section 375) defines rape as intentional, unlawful sexual intercourse with a woman, with or without her consent under several circumstances. An offender is liable to be punished with an imprisonment of minimum 7 years to maximum 10 years and fine. Further, if the offence is committed in custody or on an expecting woman, or a woman below 12 years or gang rape, the punishment will be minimum 10 years of imprisonment. However, the definition of rape under the Indian laws does not cover forced oral sex or sodomy. These acts are separately covered under section 354, of IPC, which deals with criminal assault and outraging the modesty of a woman. Section 377 of IPC deals with unnatural sexual acts while Indian law does not recognize forced sexual intercourse by a man with his wife, above 15 years, as an act of rape.

http://www.pathlegal.in/legal_services/criminal/rapelawinindia.php

Sexual Harassment

As per Indian Laws, sexual harassment can be defined as acts such as unwelcome sexual gesture or behaviour whether directly or indirectly, sexually coloured remarks, physical contact and advances showing pornography, a demand or request for sexual favours, any other unwelcome physical, verbal/non-verbal conduct being sexual in nature and passing sexually offensive and unacceptable remarks. The critical factor is the unwelcomness of the behavior, thereby making the impact of such actions on the recipient more relevant rather than intent of the perpetrator.

Laws and Acts under the Indian Penal Code (IPC)

- Section 209: Obscene acts and songs, to the annoyance of others like:

a) does any obscene act in any public place or
b) sings, recites or utters any obscene song, ballad or words in or near any public place.
Punishment: Imprisonment for a term up to 3 months or fine, or both. (Cognisable, bailable and triable offense)

- Section 354: Assault or use of criminal force on a woman with intent to outrage her modesty.
  Punishment: 2 years imprisonment or fine, or both

- Section 376: Rape
  Punishment: Imprisonment for life or 10 years and fine

- Section 509: Uttering any word or making any gesture intended to insult the modesty of a woman
  Punishment: Imprisonment for 1 year, or fine, or both. (Cognisable and bailable offense)

The Indecent Representation of Women (Prohibition) Act (1987)

Although it is not known to have been used in cases of sexual harassment, the provisions of this act have the potential to be used in two ways:
- If an individual harasses another with books, photographs, paintings, films, pamphlets, packages, etc. containing 'indecent representation of women'; they are liable for a minimum sentence of two years
- A 'hostile working environment' type of argument can be made under this act. Section 7 (Offences by Companies)—holds

companies where there has been 'indecent representation of women' (such as the display of pornography) on the premises guilty of offenses under this act.
Punishment: Minimum sentence of two years

http://www.pathlegal.in/legal_services/criminal/sexualharassmentlawinindia.php

What the New Anti-Rape Law Actually Says:

After clearing the Lok Sabha or lower house of Parliament earlier this week, a bill to toughen India's laws on sexual offenses is being debated in the upper house on Thursday.

The bill, which will amend India's penal code and laws of criminal procedure and evidence, was drafted in response to widespread street protests after the fatal gang rape of a 23-year-old woman in Delhi in December.

Among the significant provisions of the bill, seen by India Ink, are longer sentences for sex offenders, a broader definition of rape and punishments for other sex crimes like stalking and voyeurism.

Here are some of the bill's crucial changes:

– Women's rights advocates and victims of sexual offenses have long accused a male-dominated police force of refusing to register complaints by women, and even facilitating a monetary settlement or brokering a marriage between victims of rape and the accused.

The bill lays down punishment for police officers who fail to record the initial complaint, known as the first information report, of a woman who alleges she was attacked with acid, assaulted by a man who intended to molest her or 'outrage her modesty,' stripped naked or raped. Such officers can receive jail terms of six months to two years.

– The bill creates a separate offense to address acid attacks, common in South Asian countries, especially by men who are spurned by women they express an interest in.

Under the bill, those convicted of throwing acid on a woman, causing 'permanent or partial damage or deformity,' or maiming or disfiguring her, will be punished with prison sentences ranging from 10 years to life and a fine.

With an eye to the rehabilitation of the victim, the bill says the fine should be paid to the woman as compensation.

– The bill defines sexual harassment, which includes 'physical contact and advances involving unwelcome and explicit sexual overtures,' a demand for sexual favors and showing pornography to a woman who does not want to see it. Those convicted of harassment can receive prison sentences of up to three years.

Making 'sexually coloured' remarks is also included in the definition of sexual harassment, for which the bill prescribes a prison sentence of up to a year.

– The bill criminalizes the forced stripping of women, or disrobing, in public spaces or in private confines, with a minimum jail term of three years and a maximum of seven. Under the current law, disrobing a woman is not a separate offense.

– One of the more controversial provisions in the bill is the section on voyeurism, which seeks to punish men who watch or photograph women who are conducting a 'private act,' such as bathing, using the toilet or having sex.

The bill lays down a punishment of three to seven years in prison for those convicted of voyeurism more than once.

Voyeurism is not a separate offense under the current law.

– The bill creates another new, and much-debated, offense: stalking. This provision deals with men who follow a woman and establish contact with her or attempt to do so 'to foster personal interaction repeatedly despite a clear indication of disinterest' by the woman.

E-stalking, or monitoring of a woman's activities online, such as browsing or checking of e-mail, has also been made punishable.

A man convicted of stalking once can be sentenced to a term of up to three years, and if convicted again can receive a sentence of up to five years.

– The bill expands the definition of rape to include not just penovaginal intercourse but the insertion of an object or any other body part into a woman's vagina, urethra or anus, and oral sex.

This responds to a longstanding demand of women's rights groups. The issue of rape by different means was highlighted in the Delhi gang-rape case, where an iron rod was inserted into the young woman's body.

Prison sentences for rape can range from seven years to life. The current law allows courts to hand down a sentence of less than seven years for 'adequate and special reasons,' a provision omitted in the bill.

– The bill raises the age of consent for sex to 18. This means that intercourse with a woman under 18 is statutory rape and courts conducting rape trials cannot consider whether the woman consented to having sex. It also, in effect, criminalizes consensual sex with women under 18, a subject of much controversy.

– The bill does not make marital rape an offense, ignoring a longstanding demand of women's rights advocates.

– The bill takes a tough stand on rape by public servants. Under the current law, when a rape is committed by a police officer or prison staff, those convicted can be punished with sentences ranging from 10 years to life.

The bill clarifies that imprisonment for life means the convict must remain in prison till the end of his natural life.

The bill also allows women to bring a complaint of rape against members of the armed forces.

– When a rape leaves a woman dead or in a 'persistent vegetative state,' the bill demands a minimum sentence of 20 years in prison and a maximum punishment of death. This is the first time that the death penalty is being prescribed for sexual offenses in India, which, unlike nearly all European nations, retains the death sentence, but uses it only in the 'rarest of rare cases.'

– The bill increases the minimum punishment for gang rape from 10 years imprisonment to 20 years, and the maximum punishment to life imprisonment.

– The bill provides for life imprisonment or death for repeat offenders convicted of rape and gang rape.

– The bill makes procedural changes to address concerns that women are uncomfortable or intimidated by male police officers, or are treated with insensitivity when they approach police stations to register complaints of sex crimes.
   The bill requires that all initial reports involving sexual harassment, disrobing, voyeurism, stalking, rape and gang rape be taken by women officers only.

– In order to ensure speedy trial, the bill requires that rape trials be completed 'as far as possible' within two months from the time the police file charges against the accused.

http://india.blogs.nytimes.com/2013/03/21/what-indias-anti-rape-bill-actually-says/?_r=0
Criminal Law (Amendment) Act 2013
http://mha.nic.in/pdfs/TheCrimnalLaw030413.pdf
http://en.wikipedia.org/wiki/Criminal_Law_(Amendment)_Act,_2013

Appendix 5

References

A thorough review of the available literature has led us to some surprising conclusions about the effectiveness of traditional anti-rape advice. Women are often advised to use non-aggressive strategies against sexual assault (Storaska, 1975; Channing L. Bete Co., What every woman should know about rape, 1989; Channing L. Bete Co., What women and men should know about date rape, 1989). Research suggests that this is poor advice. According to one study (Zoucha-Jensen and Coyne, 1993), women who used non-forceful verbal strategies, such as crying or pleading with the assailant, were raped about 96 percent of the time. In the same study, women who did nothing to protect themselves were raped about 93 percent of the time.

Forceful verbal resistance, including yelling and loud screaming, was more effective than non-forceful verbal resistance. These strategies were associated with completion of rape from 44 percent to 50 percent of the time (Quinsey and

Upfold, 1985). This study is particularly interesting because the data were collected from rapists in maximum security psychiatric hospitals, showing that forceful verbal strategies can be effective even against the violently insane.

Running worked even better than verbal resistance. Although researchers who relied on rape crisis center records and police records (Zoucha-Jensen and Coyne, 1993) report a 55 percent rape completion rate against those who attempted to flee, broader studies such as Bart and O'Brien (1985) indicate that only 15 percent of women who attempted to flee were raped. Running was also associated with a lower rate of injury (Kleck and Sayles, 1990; Siegel et al., 1989; Ullman and Knight, 1991).

Forceful physical resistance was an extremely successful strategy. The completed rape rate dropped to between 45 percent and 14 percent when the rapist's attempt was met with violent physical force (Kleck and Sayles, 1990; Siegel et al., 1989; Ullman and Knight, 1992; Zoucha-Jensen and Coyne, 1993). Striking was more successful than pushing or wrestling (Quinsey and Upfold, 1985). Physical resistance also appears to be more effective when assault occurs outdoors (Quinsey and Upfold, 1985).

Women are sometimes advised that fighting back will increase their risk of injury. There are two problems with this argument.

First, research shows that physical resistance does not cause further injury to the resister. While there is a correlation between resistance and a somewhat higher rate of physical injury (at most 3 percent) (Kleck and Sayles, 1990; Marchbanks et al., 1990; Siegel et al.,1989), researchers who examined the sequence of events found that injury usually occurred before resistance. In other words, resisters were not injured because they had resisted:

rather, being injured motivated them to fight back (Quinsey and Upfold, 1985). After the initial injury, forceful resistance did not increase the resister's risk of further damage.

Second, this argument overlooks the fact that a woman who does not resist is virtually guaranteed to suffer the emotional and physical injury of the rape itself. Even when resisters are injured, the injury is typically much less severe than a completed rape would have been (Kleck and Sayles, 1990; Marchbanks et al., 1990; Siegel et al., 1989; Ullman and Knight, 1991). Of those 40 percent of resisters who suffered physical damage, only 7 percent suffered injury as severe as a dislodged tooth. A woman who fights back incurs no demonstrable chance of additional injury, but she gains a 55 to 86 percent chance of avoiding rape altogether (Kleck and Sayles, 1990).

When resistance does not prevent rape it can still yield important benefits. A woman who does not resist may not be viewed as sympathetically nor her trauma be treated as seriously as one who does fight back, because nonresistance may be viewed by others as acquiescence (Galliano, Noble, Travis and Puechl, 1993). In Oregon and some other states, evidence of 'earnest resistance' is required for rape prosecution (ORS 163.305(2); Criminal Code of Oregon, 1996). Women who follow the traditional advice not to resist may find that they have no legal standing to press charges against the rapist.

Women who used knives or guns in self-defense were raped less than 1 percent of the time. Defensive use of edged or projectile weapons reduced the rate of injury to statistical insignificance (Kleck and Sayles, 1990).

While many of these strategies were very successful by themselves, combinations such as yelling and fighting or yelling, fighting and fleeing further increased the chances of avoiding rape (Bart and O'Brien, 1985).

The studies we have cited have used a wide variety of research techniques. This suggests that the effectiveness of forceful resistance against rape is a robust result.

III. Psychological benefits of self-defense training

From a health education standpoint, the clearest benefit of self-defense training is that it teaches girls and women to use the most effective means to reduce their risk of rape and avoid threats to their physical and psychological well-being. There are other reasons to take instruction in this subject as well.

Pava, Bateman and Glascock (1991) conducted an extended study of the effects of self-defense instruction on visually impaired women. All of these women had a more realistic perception of risks of crime, had improved physical skills in areas such as balance and strength, and felt less vulnerable after training. Harding and Nelson (1985) report that self-defense students become more confident, analytical, and aware. They also indicate that concrete advice and skills lead to empowerment, while vague warnings and an exclusive reliance on avoidance lead to fear. Insofar as fear is a constraint to an active and healthy lifestyle, any activity such as self-defense training which decreases fear and apprehension is beneficial (Henderson and Bialeschki, 1993).

Self-defense training has many similarities to martial-arts training. A review of martial arts and psychological health concludes that increased assertiveness, confidence, self-esteem, relaxation and concentration as well as decreased anxiety all result from such training. These effects, along with decreased aggression and better social adroitness, were apparent in two studies of adolescent boys who were exposed to relatively short courses of instruction (Fuller, 1988). Regrettably, we are aware of no comparable studies involving girls.

Perhaps the most interesting and heartening results were reported by Boudreau, Folman and Konzak (1995). Surveys of the parents of over 270 children enrolled in karate classes in Toronto suggested that while boys received significant benefits from instruction, the positive effects enjoyed by girls exceeded their own and parental expectations. There was a universal improvement in self-confidence and self-discipline. Female students experienced physical and academic improvement at a rate of about twice that of boys
http://web.cecs.pdx.edu/~tellner/sd/Review.html

Acknowledgements

The writing of this book turned out to be an extraordinary journey, which took around ten months of research, interviews and 'letting it ripen', and once it was ready to be born, the book was out in what seems like one breath.

Firstly, I would like to thank Random House India and my amazing editor Milee Ashwarya, who trusted me completely and gave me the freedom to write everything I believe in and hold important in terms of content even if it sounds unorthodox. To Trisha Bora, for her amazingly fast editing and formatting—you have done a mammoth task in record time. To Caroline Newbury for her creative genius at promotion and marketing.

The major contributor for this book is my husband Anuraag, who doubled up not only as my researcher and typist, but he also selflessly lent his body as a volunteer for all the grips, holds, and kicks in the preparation as well as volunteering to be my attacker during the photoshoot (which I am sure he regretted dearly as he suffered a number of bruises and scratches). Your support has been tremendous and you are the main reason this book came together so quickly. I hope you know how much your unconditional support and love means to me. Love you!

To Rajiv Luthra, for his selfless help for putting me in touch with quite a few amazing people from the police, security experts, giving me his legal opinion on the subject of the book and extending the help of his law firm for information about procedures, the Amended Criminal law, and all things related to the law.

To all the experts in the field of martial arts, security, to police officers, bodyguards, soldiers whom I spoke to over the last year; you are too many to name but you know who you are.

To my brother Goran for sharing his knowledge in martial arts, which was of immense value to me. Your guidance and practical lessons shed a new light and cleared many points.

To Tom Jacobs—it is so interesting how our paths keep on crossing even after so many years—thank you for your invaluable lessons.

To all my girls, friends, and acquaintances who trusted me enough to share their most unpleasant stories of harassment and abuse. You helped me a lot by giving me a better perspective on understanding the Indian context.

Thank you to my Indian and Bosnian families for your support and words of advice and encouragement throughout this process. Especially my daughter Daniela who patiently waited for the parts and segments to be done so she could spend time with me and in the process, learn a few useful grips and kicks.

Special thanks to Almir and Alma whose guidance and support have always been there for me.

A Note on the Author

Vesna P. Jacob, the spirit behind Vesna's wellness Clinic is a Bosnian who made New Delhi her home some eight years back. She has established herself as a premier Pilates, fitness, and wellness expert with a long list of glitterati of Delhi's political, social, and corporate spheres. As a fitness expert, she had made an appearance on many TV channels like CNN IBN, NDTV, Headlines Today and Times Now, VOI and Sahara TV. She is also a prolific writer. Her articles have been published in *Hindustan Times, Sananda, Men's Health,* and *Prevention. Work it Out Without a Workout* was her first book.